Contents

D1257020

Preface

People who teach in colleges and universities are subject-matter specialists. They are experts in their fields, and have probably been absorbed with studies in their content area for 6 to 10 years while earning college degrees. Those who teach in community colleges and technical schools are often experts plucked directly from the world of work. You are one of these people in higher education—an expert in organic chemistry, nursing, Shakespeare, medieval history, physics, Chinese, or business management.

Now, with all, or most, of graduate school behind you, or years of experience practicing your discipline in the real world, it's time for you to share your expertise in the classroom with your own students–by teaching. Very rarely do subject-matter specialists get training in the curriculum and methods of teaching. Those who have worked in business, medicine, and technical fields may have had years of content training themselves, but no training in how to teach others to do their jobs. In other words, how do you learn to be successful at college teaching?

After teaching my very first college class, I left the room thinking, "Now *this* is what I was trained to do." Having earned a bachelor's degree in Spanish, with a minor in teacher education, and having taught high school Spanish for eight years, teaching a room full of attentive college students was kind of like going to heaven. Not to mention that it was 101 and I had taught much more advanced material to my high school students.

I returned to my cubicle in the office of graduate teaching assistants to find that my colleagues were not as enthralled by their first-day experiences. Their complaints about the first day, and about much of the rest of the semester, centered not on content, but on teaching practices. "How could I have known that what I prepared would only take 25 minutes to cover?" "Three of them came late, and two others talked a lot, like I wasn't even talking." "They didn't seem to

want to participate." "I don't even remember any of their names, and I mispro-
nounced several." "I completely forgot several things I wanted to tell them."

My colleagues had all mastered Spanish beautifully, and were developing
research agendas while they pursued PhDs, but the nuts and bolts of teaching
had never been presented to them. Teaching, like any content field, has a knowledge base, and learning the knowledge base of teaching will help any instructor to teach well. It almost seems criminal to expect any expert to be thrown
into today's college classroom without any training or background in teaching
methods, classroom organization, management, assessment, or dealing with the
psyches of today's 18- to 22-year-olds.

This book is for you if you are a new graduate teaching assistant, a community college instructor, an adjunct teaching your first class, or even a new
professor who just hasn't had the opportunity to study "how to teach." The
strategies presented are both research based and from my personal experience of
teaching at the college level for over 20 years. The book will walk you through
how to become established in the classroom on the first day of the semester, and
then share methods of teaching for getting students involved in learning. As you
teach, you will find that you love your subject matter even more when you make
it come alive for others.

While there is always a debate among professional educators about whether
teachers are born or made, learning techniques and strategies to "survive" in the
classroom will allow you to learn and grow as an instructor until you develop
your own personal teaching style. By learning what other successful college professors and instructors do, you can choose the best techniques that fit your subject and your personality. If you are going to enjoy your work in any institution
of higher education, you need to master the basics of teaching. Read on!

CHAPTER 1

Getting a College Teaching Job and Expectations

It has been said that the strength of America's higher education system is its diversity. We have two-year community colleges, technical colleges, private four-year colleges, regional public universities, and huge research one institutions. The good news is that they all need instructors to teach their students. You can teach at a small private college or in a huge urban environment—it's really up to you. The key to working in higher education is your training.

Teaching Job Titles

TEACHING ASSISTANTS

Don't let the word *assistant* fool you. Teaching assistants at many universities have all of the same responsibilities as any instructor or professor when it comes to teaching classes. They don't assist anyone. They walk into class and take full charge of the day-to-day teaching, paper grading, and assignment of final grades. At some universities, a common syllabus is used for all the 101 classes, so you don't choose the text or amount of curriculum covered, but are responsible for the material. If your 101 students do not get to the end of the semester with the same amount of knowledge as everyone else, you will hear about it, probably from the people who teach 102, as well as your supervisor.

In larger institutions teaching assistants may really assist a professor, grading papers, tutoring, or providing a limited number of lectures when the professor is attending a conference. When you apply for graduate school, find out all of the expectations of the teaching assistant position before accepting the job. The advantages of an assistantship are

1. free or subsidized tuition,
2. a minimal salary to live on,
3. teaching experience on your résumé,
4. finding out if teaching is really how you want to spend your career, and
5. it's one of the most common first steps in becoming a professor.

The downside is that you have to teach and be a full-time student, going to class yourself and writing your dissertation while tending to the needs of your own students.

INSTRUCTORS AND ADJUNCTS

We all know people who teach at community colleges, private colleges, and even some universities without having earned their doctorates. Many are truly experts in their fields, having years of experience and much to offer their students. It is very common for outstanding employees from the world of work to be asked to teach their specialty—anything from entrepreneurship to nursing to lab technology. These can be very good jobs that do not require PhDs. Who is better to teach a specific job field than someone who has been successful in it?

Some people are able to secure full-time jobs as instructors and simultaneously pursue their PhD as part-time students. The plus for these jobs is that they may come with benefits. At some colleges, one may obtain a full-time instructor position without having a PhD, and no research requirement is made of the instructor. It can be a great job for the subject-matter expert who does not want to research and write. The downside is that non-PhD instructors and non-tenure-track professors may get the least desirable classes and earn less money.

Finding a job as an instructor is generally done by knowing local sources in the higher education community where you want to work. These jobs aren't usually advertised nationally. When applying and interviewing, be sure to learn the specifics of the position and how your years of experience may or may not translate into a tenure-track position.

PROFESSORSHIPS

Winning a tenure-track professorship is indeed considered the prize for all of the hard work of completing a doctoral degree. Even with a doctorate, teaching assignments vary widely from institution to institution. Some colleges require their professors to teach four classes a semester and to conduct research and write. The number of assignments and class sizes vary widely.

Winning the Job with a Good Interview

It is not easy to get a position in higher education. In addition to knowing your subject matter, you need to know how to interview. While interviews vary widely, most institutions bring the candidates in for at least an all-day interview with several constituent groups—the search committee, the chair, the dean, students, and central administration.

Be prepared for the social aspects of interviewing—dinner with the search committee, breakfast with the chair, and coffee with the entire department. Dress professionally for all events. Business casual is as casual as you should go when attending a social event, even if some faculty members are in jeans. A career suit is appropriate for the formal interview sessions. I serve on many search committees, and yes, we do discuss the attire of candidates who do not dress appropriately. For example, one candidate's first meeting with our committee was an early dinner off campus. The candidate wore khaki pants and a wrinkled shirt, which was not tucked in. By the end of dinner, we had pretty much decided he wasn't a match for our institution. First impressions matter.

BEHAVIOR-BASED INTERVIEWING BASICS

Long used in the business world, behavior-based interviewing (BBI) has made its way into the world of education (Clement, 2008). The premise of behavior-based interviewing is that past behavior is the best predictor of future performance. Savvy interviewers ask questions of candidates that assess their skills and experience with the specifications of the job, which in higher education means teaching, research and publishing, and service. Interviewers using BBI-style questions do not ask, "Tell me about yourself," but rather phrase questions that start with, "Tell us about a time when . . ." or, "Describe how you have . . ."

The search committee should have determined questions about teaching, publishing, and service in advance. Do not be surprised if members have the questions in front of them and take notes on your answers. This is actually a good sign that the interviewers are asking each candidate the same questions, making the interviews more objective. Sample BBI-style questions include the following:

1. Describe how you teach a lesson. What do your plans include? (You may be asked questions regarding active learning or the use of technology in the classroom.)

2. Tell us about a lesson that went well and why it went well.
3. Your teaching here will be (undergraduate, graduate, or both). How have you motivated students at this level to excel academically?
4. Tell us about your research and publishing agenda. What has guided your success in getting writing completed and submitted?
5. How have you involved students in your research?
6. Where have you shared your research in the past (e.g., conferences)?
7. What are ways that you have served your institution in the past?
8. Tell us about any committee work you have done.

Of course, the ultimate BBI strategy is to observe the candidate teaching. Rating instruments are generally provided to students and faculty who observe the sample lecture or lesson of candidates.

ANSWERING BBI-STYLE QUESTIONS

PAR and STAR are guidelines to help you answer questions. PAR stands for problem, action, and result. If you are asked about a concern or problem in teaching, then you should be able to talk about that problem, an action taken, and a result learned. Likewise, STAR represents situation, task, action, and result. When asked any question, a candidate who can describe his or her experience with the situation or task presented, and then describe an action and a result, reveals knowledge and experience. It is presumed that how a candidate approached the issue in the past is how he or she will approach the issue when hired, according to BBI.

Since faculty comprise hiring committees, they may not have had any training in how to interview. If a committee member asks a hypothetical question or one not posed as a BBI-style question, you can still answer the question using PAR or STAR to guide your answer. When you provide vignettes of your teaching and experience, do so with short, concise answers.

Sample interview question:

> Here at our two-year college, we get many students who feel unprepared for a four-year institution, and that may be why they have chosen us. What experience do you have teaching underprepared students and/or first-year students how to be successful in college?

Sample answer:

> As a teaching assistant at State University, I taught 100-level courses to first-year students. I realized that I needed to start each semester with explicit directions on how to complete assignments. We always

did practice problems in class. I distributed criteria sheets or rubrics for assignments. I also gave five points to students who met with me in my office for 15 minutes during the first three weeks of the semester. By building in these kinds of support, I felt I helped students learn how to do college work. I had very few students drop my course, as they learned college work was doable.

This answer is on target for that question, and should give the candidate a high rating by the interviewer. Interviewers may have rating sheets in front of them with a scale (1 to 5) or categories (unacceptable, acceptable, target) for rating responses. Again, don't worry about this, as it indicates the interviewer is striving for objectivity. Never ask to see their ratings—it's just not done.

OTHER INTERVIEW STRATEGIES AND HINTS

1. Attending professional conferences and networking is always a good strategy when job searching.
2. Read the job section of the *Chronicle of Higher Education*, online or on paper, every week. Also read the website of your professional organization for job openings.
3. Never send a cover letter or résumé out to a potential employer until at least two other people have read and edited it.
4. Follow the job description requirements with regard to the application process and the process for sending letters of recommendation. Calling and e-mailing someone who is not listed as a contact in the job description is generally not helpful and may be detrimental to your progress toward getting an interview.
5. When taking a phone call for a screening interview, be sure that you are in a quiet place with no interruptions. Make sure your outgoing voice mail message is professional, and that family or roommates take professional messages. (I know of a candidate who took a planned interview call while horseback riding. She did not get an on-site interview.)
6. Never be late to an interview. (Past behavior is the best predictor of future performance.)
7. Send e-mail or paper thank-you notes to the committee chair and/or dean immediately after the interview.

Basic Expectations

Whether you have just been hired as a teaching assistant, an instructor, or a new professor, what are the basic expectations of your job, with regard to teaching?

1. You arrive on time and prepared for each class session.
2. You have a clear, understandable speaking voice.
3. You dress professionally, within the expectations of your campus culture.
4. You teach the curriculum, not your personal opinions and worldviews on any topic.
5. You have office hours and meet with students as needed.
6. You respond to students' e-mails and calls in a timely manner.
7. You don't have a lot of student complaints.
8. You are open and receptive to having your classes observed formally and informally by colleagues and supervisors.
9. You grade papers in a timely manner.
10. Your grading is fair and based on established criteria.
11. You cover the appropriate amount of material for each course.

Organizing before the First Day of the Semester

As you prepare for the first day of the semester, read the following about getting organized for teaching. The more organized you are, the better your supervisor's evaluations and your students' evaluations will be.

Most battles are won before they are fought, because of the resources and preparation of the armies. So, there is no such thing as being over-prepared, either personally or professionally. Your evaluation doesn't start with your first formal class observation—it begins the first time you arrive on campus. Those around you are informally evaluating your attendance at, and your behavior in, the back-to-school meetings. Your department chair will notice if you are punctual or not, and your colleagues will see if you sit in the front and pay attention or if you sit in the back and read a book. Attend, be interested, and learn from the meetings. If nothing else, start learning who is who on the campus, including the office support staff/secretaries, as they can be lifesavers in the first semester.

What should you learn in the orientation meetings? There will always be more paperwork to complete in new employee orientation—W-2s, insurance, benefits, and other forms. Do them on time or you may not get your first paycheck. There will be an employee handbook and information on required office hours, the semester calendar, how to turn in grades, and technology updates. Every year things change at colleges and universities, and you need to keep up with what's happening. While new employee and back-to-school meetings may seem overly burdensome to instructors, there is a lot to know and the procedures are different on every campus. The single most important thing to learn at meetings is who to ask when you need help—and you will need help.

THE MOST IMPORTANT THINGS TO DO BEFORE CLASSES START

1. Know the campus. Get a parking pass. Find your office, get your keys, and unpack.
2. In higher ed we live through e-mail and Web-based calendars. Get connected and make sure the technology is working.
3. Find out your teaching schedule, where the rooms are, what technology is in each room where you teach, and how to use the projection system.
4. Read your student rosters. As crazy as it sounds, count the number of students on your class rosters and compare it to the number of seats in the rooms you have been assigned. It is not fair to make students sit on the floor because of a clerical error putting 32 students in a seminar room that holds 16.
5. Hopefully, the books are in for your classes. However, you are the one who has to check this. This may mean actually going to the bookstore yourself, unless you have a student assistant. Of course, you may be able to check online.
6. Find out about the syllabus templates and requirements before you start writing a syllabus. Most colleges have a required format, and if you are one of many teaching the same course, you will be required to use a common template and timeline. You can still be creative in class with a common template and curriculum.

Professionalism

Our dress, speech, and even our attendance mark us as professionals. Being prepared, being punctual, and working to help all students succeed make us professionals. We probably entered higher education because we love our subjects, and we want to share our knowledge with others. We want to write, to create, and to add to the knowledge base of our fields. Teaching will help us to share our work and will enable students to pursue worthwhile work.

Learning to teach makes our jobs so much easier. I was lucky to have studied teaching in my undergraduate and graduate work, and to have had the experience of teaching six 55-minute classes *a day* in a high school before college teaching. Those who enter college teaching without formal education training generally learn to teach informally, through experience and trial and error. However, as the knowledge base of college teaching continues to grow, the articles, books, and on-campus training continue to improve. By adding a little study of how to teach to your work, you will enjoy the teaching part of your job even more. And it all begins with a good first day of the semester.

LEARNING THE KNOWLEDGE BASE QUICKLY

Want to begin your professional bookshelf already? There is a growing body of literature about the art and science of college teaching. In addition to this book, you may want to get one or two others for your professional bookshelf. The following is a sampling of other books that will be cited throughout this text. James Lang's (2008) *On Course* provides a week-by-week guide to your first semester of college teaching. Carolyn Lieberg's (2008) *Teaching Your First College Class* is another practical book. Barbara Gross Davis' (2009) *Tools for Teaching* and Wilbert McKeachie's (1994) *Teaching Tips* are considered classics in the field. If you feel that you are teaching unprepared students, Kathleen Gabriel's (2008) *Teaching Unprepared Students* will provide an excellent overview of what you need to know in that field.

CHAPTER 2

A Successful First Day of the Semester

Methods for teaching and organizing the college classroom are well documented, creating a knowledge base. Knowing how to start the semester with a successful first day of class is a good beginning point for learning the knowledge base of teaching, because the first day sets the tone for the semester. Your students will be won over, or turned into adversaries, by much of what is done in the very first class. Noted educator Harry Wong says it best: "What you do on the first days of school will determine your success or failure for the rest of the school year. You will either win or lose your class on the first days of school" (Wong & Wong, 1998, p. 3).

Getting Ready to Teach

Your students, especially first-year and transfer students, are probably more worried than you are about the first day of class. A part of your job is getting them engaged in the class as soon as possible. You need to make the course expectations clear on the first day, while also explaining how to succeed in the class. Explaining the workload, the grading system, and the help available should lessen their fears. They want to know who you are as a person and as a teacher. They want to know that their time and tuition won't be wasted. The first day of class should focus on getting acquainted, learning the procedures of the class, and then starting the course content. Be upbeat and enthusiastic, as well as thorough and businesslike.

Hint: It takes time to write on the board and some students have trouble reading handwriting. You can prepare everything ahead of time and save yourself the time and agony of writing on the board. Most college classrooms have projection systems so that you can type up your announcements and notes on your computer and then pull them up to project for students. By using a 24-point or larger font, everyone in the room can see the visuals. If you can't rely on the Internet or campus web, type up the materials needed and print them out to project with an Elmo or similar system. Older technology means typing up notes and making transparencies to show. The bottom line is that today's students need to see material, not just hear it. A visual is worth a thousand words, and students need visual outlines to help with note taking.

PowerPoint presentations are great, but not to be overused. Also, your notes and PowerPoints can be posted on your website or your campus web. Some instructors tell students to go to the web and print materials before coming to class, so that they can concentrate on the lecture without worrying about writing every word. Other professors prefer not to post notes, citing that their students may quit coming to class if the notes are on the website. The decision is yours, based on your campus, your students, and what is being done in class. However, you must be visual to reach today's students.

Guidelines for the First Day

It works best to get to the classroom well before the students and organize it. I create an entrance table that holds the handouts to be picked up, thereby avoiding ever having to pass out papers to 20 to 40 students. If no table exists, I make two chairs or desks serve this purpose. I teach students that the routine in my class is to come in, pick up handouts on the entrance table, and read the screen for instructions. By starting the routine from the very first day, they understand it and see its value. They know what to do and it saves time. Here are some other guidelines:

1. Post your name, and the name and section of the class on the screen, so that when students walk in, they know that they are in the right place.

2. Write "Welcome" on the screen as well as directions for what students need to do immediately. Example:

> As you enter, please tell me your name. Then, pick up a syllabus, a card, and a folder from the entrance table. Fold the card so that it will stand on your desk, then write your first name on it in big letters. Add your last name and major in smaller print on the card. Write your name on the tab of the folder (last name first, then first name). Read the syllabus until class starts.

By asking students to tell you their name as they enter, you can hear how the name is pronounced and avoid the embarrassment of pronouncing it yourself.

3. When it's time for class to start—start class. Late arrivals can catch up by reading the screen.

4. For classes of 25 or fewer, have students introduce themselves with their cards, but very briefly. I tell them that they only have 10 seconds. I also tell the class that there will be a verbal quiz after all the introductions and that they can win stars if they know who is who. (Have fun with this. Make it adult-like, not like junior high.)

5. For larger classes, have students introduce themselves to three or four people around them; then we might do "stand-ups"—stand up if you are a Spanish major, stand up if you are an education major, and so forth. I stress that they should know each other for our small group work and that they should know someone to contact in case they have a question after class.

6. Collect the folders that they have written their names on and put them in a big plastic box with a carrying case, in alphabetical order. When they need to turn in assignments, I put the box on the entrance table, and they must put their paper in their respective folder. When papers are graded, the box will be on the entrance table, and they can pull their graded test or assignment from their folder. The beauty of this system is that time is never wasted by passing out or collecting papers. I put handouts in the folders of absent students, or have a teaching assistant do so in large classes.

7. After the introductions and the explanation of the folder and box system, turn to the "Today We Will" list, which is written on the board, posted on a large paper flip chart, or projected. I like to actually write this list on the board, so I can return to it even while projecting my notes. A Today We Will list is simply an outline of what we need to do. For example, for the first day, my Today We Will list says,

- See screen for instructions for card and folder.
- Make introductions.
- Turn in folders.

- Go over syllabus completely.
- Give a mini-lecture on _____.
- Complete interest inventory.
- Do you know what to read/do before the next class?

The Today We Will list is just an outline of my lesson plan. It also allows me to walk around the room, teach from the projection system, and then look at the list for what I should do next. I tend not to forget things if I have the list. As the semester progresses, the Today We Will list might contain warm-up questions that are on the next test, too. The list helps students who do arrive late or leave early, as they can see the topics and activities they missed.

8. Give a mini-lesson or mini-lecture. Let's face it; students are in college to learn, and learning should happen on the first day. Plan to give a short mini-lesson about the first reading, or to present 10 fun facts about the subject matter. For classes that last longer than 50 minutes, I even add a short student activity. Teach in a style that gets the students to see who you are and how you teach. Since I teach courses in teacher education, I often talk about my teaching career while I talk about expectations placed upon today's teachers in elementary, middle, and high schools. That way, students get to know my background and learn about the topics of the first reading they will complete. I always include stories about how times have changed and about how some things in teaching never change.

9. Give an interest inventory. Interest inventories are great for the first day of class and contain just a few questions about the student's background and interest. In one university where I taught, we called the interest inventory an APIK—a tool to assess prior interest and knowledge. In addition to giving their name and major, students can write about a hobby, interest, or goal. Don't be too personal. Asking about hometown or home country can be embarrassing to a student. It is very important to assess their previous knowledge of your subject matter. Write two or three questions about content. These could be math problems to solve, a paragraph to write, or specific history questions. Open-ended questions are useful; for example:

- What are your goals after graduation?
- What has a teacher done in the past that helped you to learn _____?
- Is there anything else that you want me to know about you and your course of study?

You can always add one fun question:

- If your theme song played when you entered the room, what would that song be?
- What is your favorite food or candy?

10. Conclude the class. Every good class has an introduction, a body, and a conclusion. I usually teach the mini-lesson, then allow the last six to eight minutes of class for the interest inventory and individual questions. This way, students don't have to wait on others to finish. While students are writing their inventories, I alphabetize their folders and put them in the box on the table; I instruct students to turn in their interest inventory as they exit. Another good closure is to ask if they know what to read/do before the next class, and if they know three people to ask about the assignment if they have a question.

SUSTAINING THE PROCEDURES AND THE MOMENTUM

Routines are not ruts. Routines provide organization and cohesion to your classes. Organized instructors and professors get higher course evaluations, too. Have a Today We Will list on the board for every class—and follow it. After you have taught a class, put that lesson plan in a binder with any handouts used and write a few words of reflection on the plan, or record all of this electronically. Even after 20 years of college teaching, my notes still include comments like, "Allow ten more minutes for this next time," "Students wanted to know more about this," or "Find a different introduction for this topic." The next semester that you teach, the same course will be 100 percent easier because of well-recorded plans with notes.

Today's college students are stressed, often by juggling school, job, and family responsibilities. While you can't fix their personal stressors, you can alleviate some stress by planning ahead. Your midterm can be a week before the midterm crunch, thus helping students. Giving assignments well in advance, and giving the grading criteria or rubric with the assignment, reduces stress since expectations are known. Telling students the topics on the exam and giving sample problems helps them to study. After all, if students know the topics and still don't do well, who is accountable? They are. Standards are not lowered when a class is user-friendly. More content can actually be covered in a user-friendly classroom because no time is wasted with complaints and justifications.

Ranting to students about their poor preparation does not help students learn. Many more students go to college now than ever before, and therefore we all encounter students whose basic academic skills seem lower than expected.

Many students who gain college admission say that they never had to study in high school. Some high school teachers have quit giving homework. Faced with these conditions, college instructors have to teach study skills, and we have to build background knowledge for our students, since they simply don't have the prerequisite knowledge and skills that we are expecting. Sometimes a quick 15-minute review of a topic will help the whole class understand the new lecture. Does this take time away from the material we desperately need to cover? Yes, but if you launch into a topic thinking they all learned the background in high school, you will lose more time when students ask questions or simply get lost than by using a mini-review. Worse yet, if half of them flunk the first test, you will be reteaching anyway. Giving a nongraded pretest or pre-quiz will help you know what they know and don't know.

SAMPLE INTEREST INVENTORY

Welcome to Class # 423

Please complete this inventory about your background and interests in _____.

Name:_____

Major: _____

Year in school: _____

Describe how this class fits into your program of study and what you plan to do after graduation.

List two major expectations you have for this class. (e.g., learn how to . . . ; become better at . . . ; decide if I want this to be my major)

How do you learn best?

What did a professor or high school teacher do in the past that helped you stay motivated to be successful in the class?

If your theme song played as you entered the room, what would it be, and why?

[Add some questions/problems that assess prior background in the field. For example, provide math problems to solve or science questions to answer; in language classes, ask questions requiring answers in the target language. Other examples follow.]

If you could interview anyone from U.S. history, who would it be and why?

If you could interview any famous author, dead or alive, who would it be and why?

SAMPLE INTEREST INVENTORY FOR FOREIGN LANGUAGE METHODS CLASS

Name: _____

Major: _____

1. I decided to major in a foreign language because . . .

2. I studied my language(s) for _____ years before college.

3. I have traveled in the following countries:

4. I want to teach my language(s) at the following grades:

5. Elementary/middle school foreign language classes would be better if . . .

6. High school foreign language classes would be better if . . .

7. I really want to teach because . . .

8. I really knew I could speak the language when . . .

9. One concern I have about my student teaching is . . .

SAMPLE CHECKLIST FOR
THE FIRST DAY OF CLASS

_____ 1. I know where the room is and have verified it has enough seats.

_____ 2. I have a key to the room (if needed).

_____ 3. The books in the bookstore are the correct ones (or the online materials are available).

_____ 4. I have the roster of students.

_____ 5. I have enough cards, folders, and syllabi for each student and extras.

_____ 6. I have markers for the whiteboard.

_____ 7. My lesson plan is ready and has an "extra" in case I have more time.

_____ 8. I have used the technology in the room and know how it works.

_____ 9. I have a Today We Will list.

_____ 10. I have an interest inventory ready to give.

_____ 11. I have a plan for introductions.

_____ 12. I am ready to explain the syllabus.

_____ 13. I am aware of announcements that need to be made from my department/dean.

_____ 14. My teaching assistants/student mentors are informed of the schedule and plans for the first day.

_____ 15. All of the visuals are ready (overheads, PowerPoints, DVD clips).

Any other reminders?

CHAPTER 3

Organizing the Curriculum

Most new instructors ask themselves, "How will I fill up three classes a week for an entire semester?" Veteran instructors ask, "How will I ever get all the content taught in only three classes a week for one semester?" In her article "There's Too Much to Teach," Jane Roland Martin (2007) talks about her research on culture and curriculum and writes, "In view of the superabundance of cultural stock, the question is not whether to transmit, but which accomplishments, practices, skills, techniques, values, attitudes, fields of knowledge, world views of the past to hand down, in what form to transmit them, and to whom" (p. 39). This question fits all who teach in higher education, as the knowledge base in the disciplines continues to grow and more information is available every day.

Lee Shulman, past president of the Carnegie Foundation for the Advancement of Teaching, writes that a knowledge base is "a codified or codifiable aggregation of knowledge, skill, understanding, and technology, of ethics and disposition, of collective responsibility—as well as a means for representing and communicating it" (2007, p. 115). Following this definition, college teachers should be teaching the knowledge base of their respective disciplines, but how much each semester?

Where Do We Begin to Decide What to Teach?

Simply put, curriculum is what we teach. The knowledge base of curriculum studies is indeed a field in and of itself. Hundreds, if not thousands, of PhDs are earned in the field of curriculum and instruction every year, and those newly minted doctorates tend to become professors of teacher education, sharing the knowledge base of this field with future elementary, middle, and secondary teachers. What do those in higher education need to know about curriculum? What do we need to consider when we sit down and start organizing the content of our courses?

A PRIMER IN CURRICULUM THEORY

Entire books are written on the subject of today's college curriculum and what colleges should be teaching. In his book *Our Underachieving Colleges*, former Harvard president Derek Bok (2006) writes about the many facets of the curriculum and how all involved in higher education should be working toward improvement. So, the first step is to ask ourselves, "What are we trying to do?"

Historically, the curriculum taught in high schools and colleges was designed to do the following:

1. Transmit the knowledge base of the past to future generations
2. Prepare students to be participating citizens in society
3. Prepare students for the workforce
4. Help students to self-actualize; to be happy, productive, individuals

The influences on what we teach are many—the national/international professional organizations influence what we teach, as do the textbook publishers. Past and current research can significantly change what we teach. The accrediting bodies that give their stamps of approval to both the institutions and individual programs have influence. While we don't like to admit it, the high school curriculum influences what we teach, as incoming students may or may not have the necessary prerequisites for our courses. Our own students influence what we teach, as they bring their own set of background knowledge and questions to the classroom. Society and its issues influence what gets taught and technology's influence is tremendous.

Even with all of these influences, most instructors come to a new institution with a strong sense of what constitutes an introductory course in their field, as well as what is appropriate for advanced course material. It can be a good idea to review the guiding principles and standards of your professional association(s) and to keep current. See, for example, the following:

National Council of Teachers of English, NCTE—www.ncte.org
National Council of Teachers of Mathematics—www.nctm.org
American Council on the Teaching of Foreign Languages—www.actfl.org

Of course, there are many highly specialized organizations by field—the sciences, history, health and physical education, business. You are probably already a member of one or two of these learned societies.

DOWN TO THE BASICS—CHOOSING A BOOK

Many students equate the curriculum of a class to what is in their textbook. They are parti v ht, as books have a tremendous impact on what gets taught. Careful consideration must be given to book selection. When you actually get to choose your own textbooks, consider the following:

1. Is the content appropriate for this level of course?
2. Does this text fit my course objectives?
3. Is the reading level appropriate? Is there a helpful glossary of terms? Is the book organized such that students can find sections easily for review?
4. What is the cost of the book? How can I help students find a book for less money (e.g., online or at a used bookstore)?
5. Is this a book used by others in the field? Am I familiar with the author's work? Do I recognize any of the reviewers? What do other professors I know think of this text?
6. Is this text politically c   in language? Are the pictures politically correct?
7. How much will I have to do to supplement this text? Is it enough for a semester?
8. Are there online resources for me? For the students? Do references include Internet sites?
9. What did last year's students say about this book?

Of course, maybe a prior question should be, do I need a textbook? In this age of fast-paced electronic materials, much can be found online. Many instructors research and gather their own teaching materials. The electronic readers, like Amazon's Kindle, may change how textbooks are purchased and read. Two keys to remember are that copyright laws are indeed federal laws and having students buy a textbook provides easy access to the material.

One of my students recently wrote on my course evaluation that she would have preferred I select the chapters out the textbook that we used, photocopy them, and then have the copy shop sell the photocopies to the students. Apparently, she had no idea about copyright laws. Her complaint was that the book was too expensive, and we didn't read *all* the chapters anyway. I'm convinced that paying royalties to the author to copy over three-fourths of a book for students would have made the cost of those photocopies more expensive than the original book!

Creating the Syllabus

"The syllabus will force you to begin thinking about the practicalities of what you must give up in order to fit within the constraints of time, place, students, available resources, and your own limitations" (McKeachie, 1994, p. 12).

In the past the syllabus was mostly just a guide for when the topics would be presented, what was to be read, and when assignments were due. Today, the syllabus is more inclusive and is basically a contract with the students, who see themselves as customers (McGlynn, 2001). The syllabus has to be crystal clear with regard to attendance and grading policies, as well as outlining academic work. McGlynn (2001) also writes that the syllabus helps us to teach students how to do well in our courses.

Stories abound about students who will try to get around any rule that is not clearly stated. The following is an example:

A student turned in a final paper and the professor recognized the text as a paper already published in the field. Obviously, this was pure plagiarism. The professor recorded a semester grade of F and told the student. The student went to the provost and said, "No where in the syllabus does it say that plagiarizing *one* paper constitutes failing the course. If I were to get a zero on this paper, my average for the semester actually goes to a C-, as my other papers, assignments, and tests were all high As. I deserve the C-." The student received the C-, and then the professors were all required to write an academic integrity policy into their syllabi, explaining what constituted cheating and plagiarism and how one falsified assignment affects the final course grade.

SYLLABI TEMPLATES

Most departments will provide you with an electronic template of the syllabus format and you will create your syllabi from that template. Why? The first reason is that colleges and universities must provide copies of your syllabi to the accrediting bodies of the college, and these now require standardization. Colleges, or schools within the college/university, must provide syllabi to the national professional associations that accredit programs, as well. Using a standardized template actually helps protect you from difficult issues, since using the institution's guidelines for academic integrity or student accommodations keeps you from having to decide every rule and consequence yourself. Look at the following standardized template for a syllabus, and consider what changes you would need for your class. Helpful hints/explanations are included in brackets.

SYLLABUS TEMPLATE

Course number—Course name (-- hours)

SEMESTER, YEAR

Date and time of course: Office:
Room and building: Phone:
Instructor: E-mail:
Office hours:

Course Description [usually from the college catalog]

Textbooks Required

Recommended Resources

Purpose of the Course [how it fits into the program of study for a major]

Student Learning Outcomes [may be determined by the department; influenced by the accrediting bodies of the university and disciplines]

Assessment Measures [have to match outcomes]

Field Experience/Clinical Practice/ Lab Work

Use of Technology

Methods of Instruction

Attendance Policy

Participation Expectations

Academic Integrity [are generally stated in a student code handbook; many institutions now require statements about specific consequences to cheating, plagiarism, and falsification of materials]

Special Requirements [may include use of appropriate safety wear in a lab, or appropriate career clothes for internships/student teaching]

Evaluation Components and Grading Scale
A total point system is used to determine your grade. The number of points you earn is divided by the number of total points available, for the percentage.

Points are earned by [list all assignments and point value]

Details for each assignment and paper will be presented throughout the semester. A brief explanation of assignments is included in the Schedule of Class Sessions.

Accommodation Statement
Students with disabilities who believe that they may need accommodation in this course are encouraged to contact the Academic Support Center in _____ as soon as possible to ensure that such accommodations are implemented in a timely fashion. As the professor of this course, I am not allowed to give specific accommodations until the student has verified a disability with the Support Center, and paperwork about the accommodation is received.

Schedule of Class Sessions

Date	Topic/Assignment/Reading/What's Due
#1 Month Day	[summary of topic/assignment, etc.]
#2 Month Day	[summary of topic/assignment, etc.]

Date and time of final exam:

Assignments and Papers [include all statements of requirements here; late paper policy, acceptance of papers online, etc.]:
Assignment #1 [description and statement that a rubric or criteria sheet will be shared later]:

Instructor's Bibliography [In some universities, this is what students use for further info. In other institutions it is the instructor's list of what they used to develop the course. Make it clear to students if, and how, they are to use this.]

HINTS FOR SYLLABUS WRITING

1. Dividing the Material

After you know the required template, sit down with a calendar and your textbook and materials. Decide how much goes into each class. Building in a catch-up day before the midterm and final can be a good idea the first time you teach a course.

2. Attendance

Most colleges and universities have developed a comprehensive attendance policy or have said it's totally up to each professor. In either case, state your expectations. I expect students to come to class. I give points for each class attended, if they attend the whole time and don't sleep. Some professors have policies of lowering letter grades for certain numbers of missed classes. *Be careful* with this policy, as lowering an academic grade for attendance will be contested by students if it is not supported by the college and not written in the syllabus. Many colleges have completely given up on attendance and determine grades simply by assignments and tests.

3. Academic Integrity

Students who cheat, falsify, copy, or plagiarize need to know up front what the penalties are for doing so. Also, we need to teach what constitutes cheating, copying, falsifying, and plagiarizing each semester, as some students really do not understand how much material they can use without citations. Electronic media and online researching have changed the whole situation dramatically.

4. Special Requirements

If you teach a lab that requires special safety equipment, you must tell students that. If your course meets off campus or even out of the building for some sessions, you must tell students that (and the college has to support that requirement). Student dress codes for internships must be spelled out in writing in the syllabus.

5. Student Accommodations

Accommodating special need students is federal law and you have to do it. Every campus has an office that coordinates this work. Students do not get accommodations (enlarged handouts, more time for assignments, computers for tests, individualized quiet rooms for tests) unless they document their disability to the appropriate office. Once the office approves a student's special need, then the office will work with you about appropriate accommodations. You still need a statement in your syllabus.

6. Grading

See the chapter on assessment and grading in this book to develop your grading plan. Write the plan succinctly into your syllabus. Remember, once the plan is in the syllabus, it's a contract with the student. This may be the most important part of the syllabus.

7. Availability of Syllabus

Most institutions ask that professors post syllabi electronically, even if they still distribute paper copies on the first day of class. Follow your institution's policy and make the syllabi readily available to the students all semester.

SAMPLE GRADUATE SYLLABUS

EDU 603—Curriculum Theory (three hours)

SPRING, 20--

Day, time: Tuesdays, 5–8 P.M.

Classroom: Cook 110

Instructor: Dr. Mary Clement

Home e-mail:

Office: Cook 249

Phone:

E-mail:

Office hours: Mondays, 12–4:30 P.M.; Tuesdays, 12–3:30 P.M.; Thursdays 12–2 P.M.

Course Description [from the graduate catalog]

Advanced study and critical analysis of the learning environment in P–12 schools and the relationship between curriculum construction in the context of school reform. Includes study of theorists in field, the historical traditions of school practice, and the scope and philosophies of curriculum aims. Local, state, national, and international aspects of curriculum development and testing presented.

Textbooks Required

Ornstein, A. C., Pajak, E. F., & Ornstein, S. B. (2007). *Contemporary issues in curriculum* (4th ed.). Boston: Pearson/ Allyn & Bacon. *Note the year and edition.*

There will be many class handouts. Keep a notebook of them to prepare for the final and to review for your oral exam.

Purpose of the Course

This course is designed for students in the master's program. The objectives of educating the head, the heart, and the hands are followed, as outlined in the graduate catalog. The purpose of the course is to guide new and practicing teachers to be developers of human potential with regard to the development, implementation, and assessment of curriculum in the schools.

Student Learning Outcomes (Numbers in parenthesis reference the Charter School of Education program goals and the national INTASC goals.)

1. The student will study the definition and foundations of curriculum and how that background applies to today's learners. (2)
2. The student will understand the context and variables involved in curriculum development. (2, 3)

3. The student will become more competent in the development and implementation of curriculum. (4, 5)
4. The student will learn about appropriate assessment and evaluation of ongoing curriculum. (7)
5. The student will learn about the world and workplace of the teacher and ways to assume leadership roles in that workplace, especially with regard to curriculum design and programming. (7, 9)

Assessment Measures
1. The student will write a paper about curriculum in a narrative style (for first paper due, see syllabus).
2. The student will develop a model curriculum in the form of a curriculum map for a given subject/grade area (assignment sheet and grading criteria provided in class).
3. The student will use appropriate curricular vocabulary for a lesson plan and reflection on their teaching of the curriculum in the Evidence of Clinical Practice Impact on Student Learning (assignment sheet and rubric provided in class).
4. The student will write a final exam paper where the work of curriculum theorists is compared and contrasted and relate that theoretical work to their classrooms (assignment sheet and rubric provided in class).

For all of the above assessment measures, a 74% is a satisfactory score, which merits a C for the assessment.

Field Experience/Clinical Practice
Students in this class who are practicing teachers will apply the assignments to their current classrooms. Those who are seeking teacher certification will take EDU 605 concurrently and be assigned a field experience. There will be an assignment relating to the impact of your teaching on students.

Use of Technology
Students will spend one class in the computer lab to review online applications of curriculum maps. Students may choose to make their own curriculum maps using models/templates found online, or may create their own form.

Methods of Instruction
Presentation, lecture, active learning, cooperative group work, questions, discussions, modeling, role-play.

Attendance Policy
Students are expected to attend each class session and to attend the entire class session. You will earn two participation points for each class meeting that you

attend and in which you participate. For severe illness (more than two absences), please see the professor. Arriving late or leaving early will not enable students to earn full points for that class.

Academic Integrity

Your work is expected to be your own. Please see the Campus Code for a complete statement of the college's policies. If a student does not follow the Academic Integrity Policy set by the Campus Code, then the professor will inform the appropriate department chair(s), dean(s), and college provost.

The assignment, paper, or test for which the Academic Integrity Policy is broken can result in a 0 (zero) for that assignment. Receiving a 0 (zero) on a major paper, assignment, or test may result in a student failing a course, depending on the grades for all other work in the course.

Special Requirements

A paper, a curriculum map, an evidence of learning assignment, and a final exam.

Evaluation Components and Grading Scale

A total point system is used to determine your grade. The number of points you earn is divided by the number of total points available, for the percentage. Based on the percentage, grades are assigned as follows:

94–100% = A	233–248 points
90–93% = A-	223–232 points
87–89% = B+	216–222 points
84–86% = B	208–215 points
80–83% = B-	198–207 points
77–79% = C+	191–197 points
74–76% = C	184–190 points
70–73% = C-	177–183 points
67–69% = D+	166–176 points
64–66% = D	159–165 points
60–63% = D-	149–158 points
0–59% = F	0–148 points

Points are earned by

Participation	28 points
What we teach/curriculum narrative	40 points
Curriculum map	60 points
Evidence of clinical practice report	40 points
Final exam (take-home)	80 points
Total	248 points

Details for each assignment and paper will be presented throughout the semester. A brief explanation of assignments is included in the Schedule of Class Sessions.

Accommodation Statement
Students with disabilities who believe that they may need accommodation in this course are encouraged to contact the Academic support center in Krannert Room 339 (ext. 4080) as soon as possible to ensure that such accommodations are implemented in a timely fashion.

Schedule of Class Sessions

Date	Topic/Assignment/Reading/What's Due
#1 Jan. 22	What is curriculum? Video: History of curriculum.
#2 Jan. 29	Philosophy, goals, objectives of curriculum/Nel Noddings on curriculum Read Ornstein book, Chapters 1, 2 (pgs. 5–21); bring book to class to read Noddings article in class

Assignments and Papers
ALL PAPERS MUST BE TYPED. SPELLING AND GRAMMAR COUNT!! SOURCES MUST BE CITED. We are using APA, 5th edition. Late papers are only accepted up to two classes late. Ten percent is deducted for each class for which a paper is late, but after two classes the grade is a 0 (zero).

Assignment #1: What we teach and why we teach it!
The local newspaper needs a paper from you (minimum of two pages/maximum of three) that outlines what YOU teach and why. Explain the curriculum to the general public, emphasizing why you teach what you do. In writing this paper you are writing a narrative of the curriculum, including the why. (Using school mission should help you narrow your focus. Knowing what you are preparing students for should help you, also. Mentioning national, state, and district guidelines can really help the public understand where the curriculum originates.)

If you are new to teaching, your paper will be "What I will teach and why." You should discuss the same topics as listed above.
40 points

Assignment #2: Curriculum mapping
Pages: 6
Points: 60
For this assignment, you will make an outline of six weeks, nine weeks, or a semester in one subject and grade. Your curriculum "map" may look like the style of Heidi Jacobs, or may be in an outline, but should include topics, objectives or skills, major learning experiences, assessments, and resources. The map should list which topics are covered when.
More info and rubric provided later.

Assignment #3: The evidence of learning record
For this assignment you will need to teach a class, and reflect thoroughly on what the students learned. Rubric and more info provided in class.

The *final exam* will be given out at least two weeks before it is due and it will be a take-home paper where you prove you have read the chapters from the book—keeping up with the readings and taking good notes in class will help you organize for the final.

Instructor's Bibliography

SAMPLE UNDERGRADUATE SYLLABUS

EDU 405 and 505 B—Instructional Management MG, Sec., P–12 (two credit hours)

FALL, 20--

Day, time: Mondays, 6–7:40 P.M. Office: Cook 249
Classroom: Cook 104 Phone:
Instructor: Dr. Mary Clement E-mail:
Home e-mail: Office hours: Mondays, 10:30 A.M.–1:45 P.M.;
Tuesdays, 12–3:45 P.M.; Wednesdays
10:30 A.M.–1:30 P.M.

Course Description
Accompanies fall semester of senior-year experience. Applications of various techniques and approaches to organizing, managing, and adapting curriculum materials and the learning environment to meet the needs of diverse learners (including exceptional and LEP students). Development of personal plans for implementing instructional management.

Textbooks Required
Canter, L., & Canter, M. (2001). *Assertive discipline: Positive behavior management for today's classroom* (3rd ed.). Los Angeles: Canter. (MUST USE 3RD EDITION.)

Jones, F. (2007). *Tools for teaching* (2nd ed.). Santa Cruz, CA: Jones. (MUST USE 2ND EDITION.)

Purpose and Nature of the Course
This course is designed for undergraduates and graduates participating in student teaching and graduate students completing internships. The purpose of the course is to familiarize students with a variety of approaches to classroom management and to help each student develop his or her own plan for management and active learning.

Student Learning Outcomes (Numbers in parenthesis reference the Berry College and national INTASC program goals.)
The students will

1. become familiar with the theorists and current writers in the field of classroom management. (5)
2. become aware of the importance of active learning strategies, thorough lesson plans, and engaging teaching in establishing positive classroom management. (4, 5)
3. learn multiple strategies for setting up, organizing, and becoming established in one's first classroom. (5)
4. know what constitutes a classroom management plan and how to implement one. (5)
5. examine direct and indirect teaching methods, as well as methods for group work. (4)
6. learn about the differences in classroom management and discipline, as well as become familiar with the history and current law on discipline in Georgia classrooms. (5)
7. become more familiar with both academic and behavior assessments in the classroom. (8)
8. be aware of ways to build strong communication with parents, colleagues, and administrators. (10)

Assessment Measures
By the end of the semester, students will be able to

1. write lesson plans that include management strategies (lesson plan).
2. write a personal management plan.
3. practice classroom organization and routines in their field experience (evidenced in lesson plan).
4. observe, discuss, and reflect on a variety of methods used in today's classrooms, understanding the theoretical, historical, and legal issues associated with those methods (evidenced in lesson plan).
5. practice the assessment of student's academic and behavioral achievements (evidenced in reflection piece of lesson plan).
6. communicate with parents through letters, phone calls, and conferences (letter).

Field Experience/Clinical Practice
Students in this course must teach two lessons in their field experience placement. Each lesson must be observed by a cooperating teacher, school or college supervisor, or other certified teacher.

Use of Technology
Students will use word processing for assignments. Many websites will be shown and discussed in class for their usefulness with regard to classroom management.

Methods of Instruction
Presentation, lecture, active learning, cooperative group work, questions, discussions, modeling, role-play.

Attendance Policy
Students are expected to attend each class session and to attend the entire class session. You will earn two participation points for each class meeting that you attend and in which you participate. For severe illness (more than two absences), please see the professor. Being late does not give you full points. Two "lates" equal to minus one point, or leaving early twice means minus one. Missing more than 15 minutes is a minus one point. All rules of the Viking Code apply.

Being at school, a parent open house, an SGAE meeting, or other functions are NOT excused absences, whether you are a full-time teacher or a student teacher. You have to attend class.

Students who do not participate—who knit or grade papers or never have the text to follow—will not earn participation points either.

Academic Integrity
Your work is expected to be your own. Please see the Viking Code for a complete statement of the college's policies. If a student does not follow the Academic Integrity Policy set by the Viking Code, then the professor will inform the appropriate department chair(s), dean(s), and college provost.

The assignment, paper, or test for which the Academic Integrity Policy is broken can result in a 0 (zero) for that assignment. Receiving a 0 (zero) on a major paper, assignment, or test may result in a student failing a course, depending on the grades for all other work in the course.

Special Requirements
Students will write a personalized management plan, teach and reflect on lessons, and take a midterm and final exam.

Portfolio component: Assignments from this class fit goals 4, 5, and 10 for your portfolio, and may fit others.

Evaluation and Grading/Special Requirements
A total point system is used to determine your grade. The number of points you earn is divided by the number of total points available, for the percentage. Based on the percentage, grades are assigned as follows.

The +/- scale:

94–100% = A	198–211 points
90–93% = A-	190–197 points
87–89% = B+	183–189 points
84–86% = B	177–182 points
80–83% = B-	169–176 points
77–79% = C+	162–168 points
74–76% = C	156–161 points
70–73% = C-	148–155 points
67–69% = D+	141–147 points
64–66% = D	135–140 points
60–63% = D-	127–134 points
0–59% = F	0–126 points

Note: students must earn a C or better in this class for teacher education. A C- does not count as a C.

Points are earned by

Participation	26 points (Two lates will mean minus 1 point/missing more than 15 minutes is minus 1)
A student interest inventory	20 points
One lesson plan with reflection	20 points
Midterm	60 points
Parent letter with management plan	25 points
Final exam	60 points

Details for each assignment and paper will be presented orally throughout the semester. Criteria for assignments are included after the Schedule of Class Sessions. DO NOT COMPLETE ASSIGNMENTS WITHOUT REFERRING TO THE GRADING CRITERIA FOR THAT ASSIGNMENT!

Accommodation Statement
Students with disabilities who believe that they may need accommodations in this course are encouraged to contact the Academic Support Center in Krannert 329 (ext. 4080) as soon as possible to ensure that such accommodations are implemented in a timely fashion.

Schedule of Class Sessions

Date	Topic/Assignment/Reading/What's Due
#1 Aug. 25	Getting started/interest inventories

Assignments and Papers

ALL PAPERS MUST BE TYPED!! SPELLING AND GRAMMAR COUNT!! Double space and use a 12-point font. The standard 10% is subtracted for each day a paper is late. A paper is DUE the night of class and it is due in the form of paper copy. E-mailing doesn't count. DON'T E-MAIL PAPERS! TURN THEM IN ON PAPER.

Assignment: The student interest inventory
The student interest inventory is worth 20 points. You will earn the points for the following:

- A one-page interest inventory with at least eight questions (2 points each). At least two questions must address content material. This should fit on one page and be ready to photocopy and use in your classroom next year.
- The last 4 points are for a one-half page typed explanation of how you will use the interest inventory and why you chose some of the questions. Explain how this inventory will help you manage the class. If you teach non-readers/writers, explain who will administer the survey and how—especially if you teach pre-K, K, or a class with ESOL/ELL students (P–12 majors).

Assignment: The management plan
Your paper should be a minimum of two pages (12-point font). The papers should be double-spaced and written for the audience—parents and guardians (you decide how to address the letter). If at all possible, you should actually use these letters this year or next. In addition, they may fit objectives for inclusion in your portfolio. Your paper is worth 25 points, as per the syllabus.

For this letter, you may choose the beginning of the school year, or you may make the letter current. Start by saying something positive about the year, the school, the class, and so forth (5 points). Then explain your philosophy of classroom management (5 points), perhaps explaining why management is different than discipline! After a page of narrative, include your page of classroom rules, supportive feedback, and corrective actions (or positives and consequences, you decide on the wording) (10 points). Do you want parents to respond, and if so, how?

The last 5 points are for grammar, punctuation, and clarity.

IF YOU PLAN TO USE THESE LETTERS, or any others, remember to first share them with your mentor and principal (interns) or cooperating teacher.

Instructor's Bibliography

CHAPTER 4

Lessons, Assignments, and Grading Criteria

Long gone are the days when a professor could walk into a classroom and say, "Now, where did we leave off?" or announce to the class that they should "write a paper." Today's students want, and need, structured lessons with beginnings, middles, and ends. They demand criteria for assignments—criteria that explicitly state expectations and what they must do to earn the desired grade. While some educators lament this accountability to the student, bemoaning the fact that this takes the creativity out of classes and assignments and promotes working for the grade and not learning for the sake of learning, the accountability works both ways. If students know in advance what is expected in class and on assignments, the responsibility for producing the work is theirs.

Lesson Planning

According to an old adage, "Failing to prepare is truly preparing to fail." That is why we plan lessons. Think back to some of your own college classes. Can you remember classes where the professor seemed fully prepared for the day's lesson? Did he or she plan lectures, discussions, and activities that reinforced what you read? Did the instructor know if you were learning the material *before* the major exams? Did you learn more in classes where the instructor did these things than in some other classes? If you have even the smallest feelings of fear when you think about stepping in front of your classes and filling up the class time, then you see the need for lesson planning.

First of all, lesson plans vary widely in format. Kellough and Carjuzaa (2006) write that

> a written lesson plan should contain the following basic elements: (a) descriptive data, (b) goals and objectives, (c) rationale, (d) procedure, (e) assignments and assignment reminders, (f) materials and equipment, (g) accommodations for students with special needs, (h) a section for assessment of student learning, and (i) reflection on the lesson, and ideas for lesson revision. (p. 145)

Barak V. Rosenshine wrote a six-step guide that for years served as a lesson plan to many practicing teachers in kindergarten to grade 12. As you read his steps, ask yourself if this is how you were taught mathematics or any other subject:

1. Daily review, checking previous day's work, and reteaching
2. Presenting new content/skills
3. Initial student practice
4. Feedback and correctives (and recycling of instruction as needed)
5. Independent practice so that students are firm and automatic in skills
6. Weekly and monthly reviews (as cited in Ornstein, Lasley, & Mindes, 2005, p. 197)

Another pioneer in the knowledge base of lesson planning was Madeline Hunter, who is credited with the following seven-step lesson plan:

1. Anticipatory set (focuses students on what will be learned)
2. Objectives and purpose (explicitly informing students of what they will learn)
3. Input (teacher provides information in a variety of ways)
4. Modeling (teacher models writing, problem solving, etc.)
5. Checking for understanding
6. Guided practice (of new knowledge or skill)
7. Independent practice (Hunter, 1994)

As you read any of these examples, you may see a model that works well for your discipline. My own lesson plan template follows:

LESSON PLAN TEMPLATE

Topic:

Pages of book/online readings for reference:

Instructor's goal(s): The instructor will present, introduce, or review . . .

1.

2.

Student objectives: By the end of this class, the student will . . .

1.

2.

   I. Focus/review/introduction/attention grabber

  II. Body of lesson

     1. The instructor lectures, presents, models, explains, questions . . .

     2. The student answers, discusses, solves problems . . .

     3. The instructor . . .

     4. The student . . .

     Repeated for length of class.

 III. Review/conclusion/assessment of student learning

     Examples:

     1. One-minute paper on clearest and muddiest points

     2. Solve two problems

     3. Questions and answers

 IV. Extra materials, questions, problems, if time permits

  V. Resources and materials to take to class

 VI. What do I need to change for next time? Reflection.

When asked if I really do write lesson plans the way I teach others to write their plans, I respond, "yes." I also tell my students that if I don't have a typed plan for class, they don't have to stay, because I feel planning really is that important. Do I change plans while teaching? Absolutely—as the students' learning and their questions lead us. I write out a one-page lesson plan for each hour I teach, and the plan emphasizes the introduction, the body, the conclusion, and the extras. I write a short outline of what students are to learn on the board (the objectives) or on a piece of chart paper, so that students know what they are to learn.

I encourage teachers of any subject or level, including those who teach graduate courses, to always think deeply about what they want to happen in every class they teach. If we as instructors don't know what we want to happen and don't plan for what we do and what we want the students to do, then there is no way the learning will just happen. Good teaching is purposeful. Effective teaching is explicit with goals and objectives.

"A goal is what the teacher wants to accomplish in a given class. . . . Goals are written with words like present, introduce, model, interpret, read, demonstrate, clarify, and review" (Clement, 2005, p. 8). Every class needs one to three goals. By being as specific as possible with your goals, your plan will take shape more easily. For example, here are some goals for an English literature class:

1. The instructor will (TIW) describe the history of the time when the piece was written.
2. TIW provide definitions of key vocabulary.

The objectives follow the goals, but state what the students should know or be able to do by the end of the class. For example:

1. The student will (TSW) be able to explain four examples of how the novel deals with the issues of the time in which it was written.
2. TSW be able to define the 10 most commonly used words unique to the vocabulary of the piece.

Obviously, tests and final papers are then written to the students' learning objectives. In fact, when we write the objectives and topics of a lesson on the board, we are telling the students in each class what will be on the next test. A test written for the objectives taught is a criterion-referenced test. (More about these in the chapter on assessment.)

FOCUS/REVIEW/INTRODUCTION/ATTENTION GRABBER

Some people call the focus activity a sponge, as it soaks up time until all students are seated and class begins. We have a focus in every lesson to get students thinking about our discipline, and not about their own personal issues. Students don't just come into class, sit down, and look at us with a longing to learn all about the new topic. Rather than expecting students to say, "Teach me all about international trade agreements," we need to get them thinking about how international trade agreements affect them personally. With regard to international trade agreements, try writing this focus on the board: "List all the items you have with you, or on you, that were not made in America." Students should learn the routine that every class starts with a focus—and that the focus topics and questions lead to exam questions.

THE BODY OF THE LESSON PLAN

The body of the lesson plan is its heart—what you do to teach the material in a way such that the students can learn it. Several chapters of this book are devoted to teaching methods, and the methods will be used in the body of the lesson. Variety is important to teaching, as is teaching that is verbal and visual. For centuries college professors just talked and students were expected to learn. While lecturing has its place in higher education, today's students need visuals and chances to interact and practice to learn. As Fred Jones writes (Jones, Jones, Jones, & Jones, 2007), we have to practice say, see, and do teaching, because students learn by hearing, seeing, and doing. Other educators talk about hands-on and minds-on learning. In other words, whether the body of a lesson is a lecture, a lab, a role-play, a discussion, or a video teleconference, students have to be engaged.

CONCLUSION/REVIEW/INFORMAL ASSESSMENT

Lessons need to be given closure—and not just the standard "We're out of time, see you next class." A good closure helps you to assess how much the students have learned, helps to "set" the material in the students' minds, and should be an advertisement for the next class. Yes, we do have to promote our own classes so that students attend. When I taught college-level Spanish, I would do a promo like, "Next class we will learn all about the subjunctive. If you attend, I guarantee you will understand it and do better on the exam. Miss class and the subjunctive will always be a mystery."

How do we make reviews, closures, and assessments simple and meaningful? Ungraded two- or three-question quizzes can help us assess. Sometimes go over them as a class in the last two minutes, or you can read them yourself, providing the answers the following day.

The instructor doesn't have to lead the review. Have the students do it. By asking students what they learned and what they still want help with, you can get some pretty good feedback. Make it a formal part of the lesson, not something you are trying to do while students are packing up and walking out the door.

Teaching Classes That Meet in Blocks/Blocked Time Frames

I have taught three-hour evening classes for graduate students in teacher education for the past 12 years. I'd like to share the four-part plan I've developed that keeps students engaged at the same time it provides a robust intellectual experience. It's another spin on how to prepare a lesson.

1. GET THEM IN, GET THEM FOCUSED

My first goal is to get students thinking about the class, not about their bad day at work or what their children are doing at home. I set up the room before class starts. I post a list of everything we will do in the next three hours, so students know how much there is to accomplish and so that late arrivals or those who leave early know that they missed something. There is always a tough, thought-provoking question on the screen. It may review reading material or end up on an exam—all of these questions are important and guide the rest of the session. The students start class by answering the question. They may write or think about the answer—either way, I start class with their answers.

2. PRESENT/LECTURE/EXPLAIN

After the opening discussion I present the new material for that session. Most weeks, my students are assigned two or three chapters or articles to read before class. I tell them to bring the readings; in class we "bring them to life." When I can, I project the author's picture on the screen, or show a video clip of the author discussing his/her work. Many authors now have these clips on their websites or on YouTube.

After a video clip, I project my notes on the screen, stating that they don't have to wonder what I wanted them to get out of the reading, as I will tell them. However, frequently my notes are questions or re-directs back to the reading: "Go to the third paragraph on page 317, reread it, and explain the author's opinion in your own words." I also challenge students to question a writer's research or background: "Having read this seminal work by author X, what critiques do you have about his/her research? List three." Frequently they discuss their answers with a partner, which helps to break up the long class period. Some students report on these exchanges in the whole class discussion that follows. This gives me an opportunity to elaborate or add points they may have missed.

3. APPLY

Students need to thoroughly understand new material before they are asked to apply it. Generally those applications occur in small groups. After students read about the sources of high school curricula, I might ask groups to design a curricular change in their schools. They find directions and relevant questions on the screen. Authentic tasks work best. If the groups are doing something members see themselves doing in the future, they see the work as relevant and tackle the exercises with enthusiasm. I don't grade this group work, using it instead as a springboard for discussion and means to promote collegiality and brainstorming. An activity like this might occur just before students write a paper about the same or a related task.

4. REVIEW, CONCLUDE, AND ASSESS

I might use an activity to end class. I put up large posters around the room, each with the name of a theorist we have studied recently. I ask students to go to two of the posters and write their most vivid memories of that theorist. They cannot repeat what others have written. As they write, I walk around the room and talk with students, providing individual attention and answering questions.

I may use a short reading that summarizes, adds to, or is related to the lecture. Students read this handout and then tell me why I chose that reading for my conclusion. I am most pleased when a student observes, "This says it all. Why didn't we start here?" My response, "You wouldn't have known it said it all if we hadn't studied it all during the last three hours!"

Here are a few other keys to success:

- Explain when the breaks are—and you must have breaks for blocked classes.
- Students need drinks and food. Since I do not teach in a lab, I encourage students to bring drinks, snacks, and even a lunch that they can eat during the break and finish as we are working.
- Start and end on time. I find it helps to keep the list of what we must accomplish visible throughout the session. Students can see how much we've done and what still remains.
- Spend time letting students get acquainted during the first couple of classes. Building the class community will help throughout the semester.
- Walk to the back of the room before class starts and see if you can read whatever you have posted easily.

There is no such thing as being over-prepared. My four-step plan takes time to prepare, but it benefits students in ways that make it worth the effort.

Preparing Assignments

Veteran professors have often been heard to say, "It's tougher to teach today's students because they have been completely spoon-fed until college." Those same professors may continue to say that they would never tell a student exactly how many pages to write for their paper, or which questions to answer in an essay, or exactly how many points will be taken off for spelling and grammar. Well, today's students may have been spoon-fed, but they do demand the criteria for their assignments and papers. By making the criteria known and having a "no mystery" approach, students have the responsibility on them for the quality of their work.

The following is an assignment I used to give orally by just telling students their assignment was a paper about how to impact student learning and raise achievement scores. Now, I give them a two-page criteria sheet that lists expectations.

I found that when I gave the criteria sheet, I got all the parts of the assignment that I expected. No student could say, "But I didn't hear you say I had to include two lesson plans or a unit plan." If I did receive a weak assignment, I put another copy of the criteria sheet on the student's paper, with my comments of where they lost points. Students quit arguing with us over grades when we are this clear. Well, most do!

IMPACT ON STUDENT LEARNING PAPER CRITERIA SHEET

[Second assignment in teacher education course]

1. As teachers, we are often asked to raise student achievement. Identify one area where your students need help to improve achievement. What data drives your decision? (Pre-tests? Standardized scores of last year? Other?) *3 points*
2. Once the area of improvement is identified, how do you think you could raise achievement? In other words, what has to change? For this part of the paper, the change must be curricular. Identify the change specifically, such as books, a change of sequence of material, or a change of time allotted for topics. *3 points*
3. Next, you must include an instructional change that accompanies the curricular change outlined in step 2. If you change the time allotted, for example, share a specific instructional change that makes better use of time. (Refer back to authors we have read. Cite at least one author.) *3 points*
4. What costs are associated with the above instructional and curricular changes? What would your newly implemented changes look like in your classroom? Are there any obstacles besides cost? What about administrative or collegial support? *3 points*
5. Cite at least one theorist we have read who supports/encourages the curricular or instructional change you advocate. *2 points*
6. Now, outline how you would assess the results of your change to prove effectiveness. *3 points*

Length: To answer the above, the minimum length is three pages. *8 points*

Now, you need to include at least two lesson plans that address the specific curricular and instructional changes you have outlined above. Each plan must be a minimum of one and one-half pages.

OR

Include a three-page unit plan (see sample) that outlines the changes you wish to make. *10 points*

Grammar, spelling, clarity. *5 points*
Total: 40 points
To check yourself:

1. Paper is at least three pages long.
2. Two plans or a three-page unit plan attached.
3. Someone else has read my paper for clarity, spelling, etc.

Rubrics and Templates

For another assignment in a teacher education class, I put a template of the assignment on the web. Students get the template, write the necessary information, and then turn the assignment in. Explanations are included for certain areas of the assignment. A complete rubric for the assignment appears in table 4.1. This type of assignment is typical of the type of documentation some K–12 teachers must now do for assessment of their own teaching and their impact on student learning, by the way.

WHY USE RUBRICS?

First, a rubric is a way to grade using categories of criteria and quality indicators. Rubrics are easy to write; just decide in advance what is expected in the assignment or paper, then decide the quality indicators and how many points will be awarded for each (or use a website like www.rubistar.com). Again, this eliminates the problem of sitting up all night with papers and saying, well, how much did I take off for that mistake last time I saw it? A rubric makes grading less subjective, and students have less to argue about if they know the expectations before writing the paper and then don't follow through. And yes, *always* give the rubric with the criteria sheet, or make the rubric the criteria sheet and give it to students with the initial assignment. Some professors include the rubrics in their syllabi. A rubric does not have to be a whole-page document and may look very simple, like table 4.2.

The short paper graded by this rubric is worth only 16 points. A student who turns in six paragraphs that address three issues and have two grammar errors and four spelling errors would earn 8 points, or only 50 percent. Some professors would copy the rubric and circle the points as the feedback for the paper. This may seem brutal, but it is crystal clear how the points were derived. Obviously, a term paper would have a much longer and more involved rubric.

As the instructor, you decide how many points for each category. Having a rubric should not take away from the creativity of the paper, but should help the student organize and prioritize his or her writing. Math problems fit a rubric well, as points can be given for answers and work shown. A science experiment fits as each step earns a certain number of points.

The criteria sheet or rubric helps a student see the expectations for the assignment. Only when students know the expectations can they hope to achieve them. As the instructor, creating the criteria sheet and/or rubric makes grading the assignments 100 percent easier, as you know what you are assessing and how much you are deducting before reading the first paper.

Table 4.1. Evidence of Clinical Practice Impact on Student Learning Rubric

Student: _____   Course: _____   Date: _____

Rating ▶ / Indicator ▼	Not Acceptable □0 / □1	Acceptable □2 / □3	Target □4 / □5	Score
Description of Activity	Minimal description of teacher or student activity and some events that does not aid in understanding of analysis and reflection.	Enough description of teacher and student activity to determine flow and aid in understanding of analysis and reflection.	Concise, yet rich description of teacher and student activity, and flow of events to support strong analysis and reflection.	
State, national standards and instructional objectives	State or national standards numbers identified. No specific instructional objectives provided. Does not explain why changes would improve student learning.	State or national standards numbers identified. Specific instructional objectives are stated but lack measurable terms.	State and national content standards are written out. Specific instructional objectives stated in measurable terms.	
Pre-condition(s) of Students	Minimal contextual factors and pre-assessment descriptors indicate teacher displays little or irrelevant knowledge of students' skills and prior learning related to standards and objectives.	Contextual factors and pre-assessment descriptors indicate teacher's general knowledge of students' skills and prior learning related to standards and objectives.	Contextual factors and pre-assessment descriptors indicate teacher's general & specific understanding of students' skills and prior learning related to standards and objectives.	

(continued)

Table 4.1. Evidence of Clinical Practice Impact on Student Learning Rubric (Continued)

Student: _____   Course: _____   Date: _____

Rating ▲ Indicator ▶	Not Acceptable ☐0 ☐1	Acceptable ☐2 ☐3	Target ☐4 ☐5	Score
Post-condition(s) of Students	Assessment contains no clear criteria for measuring students' performance relative to standards or instructional objectives.	Assessment criteria are developed and imply linkage to standards and instructional objectives.	Assessment criteria indicators are clear and are explicitly linked to standards and instructional objectives.	
Documentation of Student Learning	Analysis of student learning is not aligned with standards and instructional objectives. Student data is not provided in graphs and tables that are clear and understandable and do not accurately represent the data. No student work samples provided.	Analysis of student learning is partially aligned with standards and instructional objectives. Student data is provided in graphs and tables that are understandable and contain few errors in representation. All student work represents similar level of proficiency.	Analysis of student learning is fully aligned with standards and instructional objectives. Student data is provided in graphs and tables that are easy to understand and contain no errors in representation. Varied example of proficiency represented in samples of student work.	
Reflection	Provides no ideas or inappropriate determination of teaching effectiveness without any relevance to theories of teaching or learning.	Provides ideas though limited determination of teaching effectiveness based on theories of teaching and learning.	Provides sound reasoning to determine teaching effectiveness based on theories of teaching and learning.	

Table 4.1. Evidence of Clinical Practice Impact on Student Learning Rubric (Continued)

Student: _____   Course: _____   Date: _____

Rating ▲ Indicator ▼	Not Acceptable □0 □1	Acceptable □2 □3	Target □4 □5	Score
Strategies for Improvement	Provides no strategies or inappropriate strategies for redesigning learning objectives, instruction, assessment, and does not explain why changes would improve student learning.	Provides strategies for redesigning learning objectives, instruction, or assessment, but offers little rationale for why these changes would improve student learning.	Provides strategies for redesigning learning objectives, instruction, or assessment, and explains why these changes would improve student learning.	
Organization	Writing is disorganized; no evidence of a logical format. Writing contains more than 3 errors in spelling, punctuation, and grammar which detract from reader's understanding.	Writing is organized, but format and structure are weak. Writing has no more than 2 errors in spelling, punctuation, and grammar.	Logical organization, using appropriate format and written structure. Completely free from spelling, punctuation, and grammatical error.	
			Total Score	

Table 4.2. Rubric for Grading a Short Paper

Criteria	Quality Indicators for Scoring			
	4 Points	3 Points	2 Points	1 Point
1. Length	10 paragraphs	8–9 paragraphs	6–7 paragraphs	< 6 paragraphs
2. Grammar	0 errors	1 error	2 errors	3+ errors
3. Spelling	0 errors	1 error	2 errors	3+ errors
4. Content clearly addresses	4 issues	3 issues	2 issues	1 issue

CHAPTER 5

Grading Policies and Test Writing

What is the source of most student complaints? Grading. Grading can be a huge source of confrontation with students and can create much personal stress for you. However, finding and using a clear grading system will save you hours of anguish. Knowing how to write objective, valid tests will diminish the student complaints and help you actually know what your students are learning.

How many times have you been in a college or graduate course where the instructor's syllabus included something like this:

Grading policy
    30% Assignments
    35% Midterm
    35% Final exam
Your scores were
    Assignments: A-, B+, A, B
    Midterm: A
    Final exam: B

What do you think your final grade should have been? An A or a B? Is the fact that you attended *every* class a deciding factor in your favor? And you sat in the front row and asked pertinent questions? Should your participation have counted?

Let's look at the same grades in another manner. The instructor's syllabus has the following:

Grading policy
    Assignments: four assignments worth 30 points each
    Midterm: 140 points
    Final exam: 140 points

Each time an assignment or test is graded, you will receive the number of points earned over the number of possible points. This translates into a percentage, which is then applied to the following scale for individual assignments. Additionally, your total points indicate the percentage and final grade as follows:

Grading scale for assignments and final grade

Scale:	Final Grade:
94–100% = A	376–400 total points
90–93% = A-	360–375 points
87–89% = B+	348–359 points
84–86% = B	336–347 points
80–83% = B-	320–335 points
77–79% = C+	308–319 points
74–76% = C	296–307 points
70–73% = C-	280–295 points
67–69% = D+	268–279 points
64–66% = D	256–267 points
60–63% = D-	240–255 points
0–59% = F	0–239 points

Your scores were

Assignments: 28/30 (A-), 26.5/30 (B+), 29/30 (A), 25.5/30 (B)
Midterm: 133/140 (A)
Final: 119/140 (B)

Your points earned: 28 + 26.5 + 29 + 15.5 + 133 + 119 = 351

Your total points (351) divided by the total possible (400) equals 87.75 percent, or a clear B+. You may use the percentage or the points listed—it's a B+. And, by the way, this still makes assignments worth 30 percent of the final grade, and each exam worth 35 percent.

Of course, this is *so much* easier if you don't use plus and minus grading, and if you avoid half-points.

Grading scale and policy

90–100% = A	360–400 points
80–89% = B	320–359 points
70–79% = C	280–319 points
60–69% = D	240–279 points
0–59% = F	0–239 points

Then, using the same earned point divided by total points, your final grade is a B.

Should participation count? Participation grades and points have been used less and less over the years, as they are subjective. If you do factor in participation points, then they must be objectively specified. For example, in the previous example, you might have 45 participation points—one for each class during the 15-week semester. The points are earned by attending and participating while in class, not sleeping, knitting, or texting. You may state that points are earned by attending and being attentive. Imagine that the previous example had 45 participation points, and the student earned 42 of them. His or her grade is now 393 points divided by the new total of 445—88 percent, or a B. It's still a B.

If the professor gives 90 participation points in the preceding example (two per class attendance) and the student attends *every* session, the student's grade is now 441 divided by 490—90 percent, or an A. Participation points can really help or hurt a student. Participation points should never be added as a bonus, or subtracted as a punishment, when a student is a few points away from a higher (or lower) grade and the instructor just "loves" or "hates" the student's behavior. Many departments have a policy on participation points. If there is no policy, ask other professors, but remember that the final goal of grading is assigning the most objective descriptor of the student's level of achievement in the class. We need to find other ways to develop students' civility in class.

Students need to thoroughly understand your grading policy and how to figure their grades. You may want to consider building a worksheet page into the syllabus about grades, or to provide the grading worksheet after the first graded assignment is completed.

"TRACKING MY GRADE IN THIS COURSE" WORKSHEET

This course has four assignments, a midterm, and a final. As each is graded, you can record your points earned and figure your grade.

Assignment 1: My score _____ / 30 possible
Assignment 2: My score _____ / 30 possible
Assignment 3: My score _____ / 30 possible
Assignment 4: My score _____ / 30 possible
My midterm grade: _____ / 140 possible
My final exam grade: _____ / 140 possible
My points earned: _____ / 400 possible = _____ %

See the scale provided in the syllabus and you know your grade.

To answer the question "If I have X points earned before the final, what is the best possible grade I can earn in the course," do the following:

Add your points, then add the possible points available on the final and refer back to the scale in the syllabus. For example, if you have earned 180 points before the final and get a perfect final exam, your grade will be 180 + 140, which equals 80%, or a B. (A B- if pluses and minuses are used.) So, no, you can't get an A.

It is hoped that the vast majority of college students would be able to read your syllabus and then figure their own grade. However, it has been my experience, and that of other professors, that many students cannot do this until we teach them how. The total point system is the most straightforward method for averaging grades. Telling students that 40 percent of their grade is based on the final exam doesn't help them know how to average their grade, as they don't know how to "weight" their grade and do the math. If you use that system, include a crystal clear explanation of how to average the final grade. First-year college students, including community college students, may really appreciate your worksheet on how to determine their grade. (I use this worksheet with graduate students, and I have gotten rave reviews about the clarity of my grading.)

As a new instructor, you may not know exactly how many assignments and quizzes you will give. You can still use the total point system without knowing the exact points by explaining the range of points that will be available. An example follows:

GRADING POLICY

Assignments: There will be homework assignments ranging from 10 to 30 points
Quizzes: There will be quizzes worth 20 to 40 points
Midterm: 100 to 140 points
Final exam: 100 to 140 points

The exact number of assignments and quizzes will be based on how the class progresses through the material. Each class is a little different. To determine YOUR grade, keep track of all the points you earn on each assignment, quiz, and exam, and then add up your points and divide by the total offered. That percentage is then applied to the 90%, 80%, 70%, 60% scale for the letter grades of A, B, C, D. A percentage below 60% is an F.

To track your grade, imagine you have earned the following points out of the possible totals:

Assignments: 12/12; 14/15; 17/20; 10/12; 22/25; 23/30; 17/20
Quizzes: 10/20; 15/20; 27/30; 35/40
Midterm: 111/130
Final exam: 110/140

You earned 423 points out of 514 possible. This is 423/514, or 82%, a B.

What determines the number of points on assignments, quizzes, and exams? The points are earned by the number of questions solved correctly, or sentences written, or lines translated, or problems solved. Yes, you may make an assignment that is not a multiple of five, or ten, or an even number, because you are using a very straightforward total point system. This system works well and gives you flexibility.

Criterion- and Norm-Referenced Grading

All of the preceding examples for grading are for mastery grading, or criterion-referenced grading. Criterion-referenced grading is also called competency-based grading, as it is based on preset standards. This means that if you feel that 90 percent of the material tested is the standard for an A, you write a test that measures the material taught, the criterion, and all students who earn 90 percent of the points on the test earn an A. Criterion-referenced grading has been the standard in grading for decades in both high schools and colleges. It is important to note that "in criterion-referenced grading, the aim is to communicate information about an individual student's progress in knowledge and work skills" (Callahan, Clark, & Kellough, 2002, p. 349).

Years ago, you may have experienced norm-referenced grading. Norm-referenced grading "measures the relative accomplishment of individuals in a group . . . by comparing and ranking students and is commonly known as grading on a curve" (Callahan et al., 2002, p. 349). With true norm-referenced grading, a small percentage of students earn As, a larger percentage Bs, and the majority of the class earn Cs, an average grade. The same number of students earn Ds as Bs, and the same number of students earn Fs as As. The use of norm-referenced grading is not supported by research and current thinking in the field of assessment. To read more about why not to use norm-referenced grading, see the work of Rick J. Stiggins and/or Thomas R. Guskey, noted writers in the field of assessment, or go to part 8 of Barbara Gross Davis' *Tools for Teaching* (2009).

Why don't students want to be graded on the curve? The answer is simple. If there are 28 students in a class, and all do the work and receive averages on the work that total above 70 percent, a large number of those students will get grades of C, D, and F. In fact, in a small graduate class of 20, norm-referenced grading will mean some students get Ds and Fs who perhaps earned 85 percent of the total points available in the course. Criterion-referenced grading, on the other hand, does not pit student against student, but rather tells a student that his or her grade is based on the amount of the material he or she learned in the course. Has criterion-referenced testing and grading contributed to grade inflation? Some argue it has, but there are other causes as well. Today's students often do not stay in a course where they anticipate a C or lower. They are allowed to withdraw at late stages in the semester in many institutions.

Sometimes an instructor returns a test and tells that class that he or she has added points to everyone's score to "curve it." If everyone missed three questions, maybe the instructor then adds the six points for those three questions to everyone's grades. This really has nothing to do with grading on the curve, but rather is just a way to improve a set of relatively low test scores. It may indicate that the test was poorly written, not covering the material of the class, or that students didn't have enough time to master some of the course material. As some professors argue, students simply didn't spend enough time practicing and studying the material independently, and the professor does not want low grades (and low course evaluations) for that class. Be careful with adding points to everyone's grade, but it is OK to occasionally remove a test question from everyone's score, or to add on a limited number of points.

We have to look at the big picture. Do we want students sitting in class scared about the competitiveness of getting a 90 percent and it not being an A or B, or do we want students to learn as much as possible and succeed? Mastery of material and success should be goals. If you feel a criterion-referenced scale is yielding too many high grades, teach more material, or make tougher tests, or change the scale to 95 percent for an A, 88 percent and above for a B, and 80 percent for a C. Obviously, if you are teaching people to be medical technicians, and those graduates are going to take my blood and monitor my surgery, I am hoping that they earned better than a 60 percent in your course on monitoring surgery. Much depends on the nature of your subject matter and the level of training required by your students.

Reliability and Validity of Grades and Exams

Since a large part of grading is based on tests, you need to know how to write valid, reliable ones. When you were a student, did you ever take a test and leave the room saying, "I didn't know to study that," or "Those questions were nothing like we did in class"? When this happens, the validity of the test or quiz is probably quite low. A valid test measures what it is intended to measure. A reliable test measures the accuracy with which a testing technique consistently measures what it is supposed to measure. For example, many people doubt that one ACT exam measures their child's readiness for college (validity). However, few doubt that the ACT is reliable, because when a student takes the test over and over, the scores are very similar each time the test is taken. It is important to know how to write tests with the most validity and reliability.

Types of Test Questions

Selection questions remain quite common in college testing. Selection questions include multiple choice, true/false, matching, and ordering. Students may like selection questions because these questions provide a chance for a right answer with a guess. However, selection questions are not necessarily easier. Tips for writing good multiple-choice questions include the following:

1. Write some introductory material, then a stem, then four responses that match the stem in grammar and in language. Example: For each statement/ question, choose the one best answer.
   The term for when a test measures that which it is intended to measure is
   a. validity
   b. reliability
   c. readability
   d. credibility
2. Vary where the correct answer is placed. There should not be patterns, such as aac, cca, or aac, for the correct answers.
3. Keep responses the same length.
4. Avoid the use of words such as always, all, never, and none (For more specifics about writing test questions, see, for example, Anderson, 2003)

Again, just as with any type of testing, students should see sample questions on a practice quiz or on the screen as warm-up discussion questions when class starts. Yes, we, the professors, have to teach students how to read and take our tests.

Why use multiple-choice questions if students call them multiple-guess questions? You can cover a lot of material with multiple-choice questions. While they take longer to write, they are much easier to score, and Scantron machines, or a computer-based test, will get you scores very quickly. With hundreds of students, sometimes this is the most efficient method.

Why use true/false questions if the student has a 50 percent chance of guessing the right answer? True/false questions can be a good choice for quick quizzes to see if students read the homework and have a basic understanding. They are easy to score, also, even without a Scantron or computer version of the test.

Fill-in-the-blank questions are halfway in between selection and longer production questions (short-answer and essay). A fill-in-the-blank question works well if there is only one answer. Example: _____ was the fourth president of the United States. Fill-in-the-blank questions become harder to grade when multiple answers are acceptable, and often many answers are indeed acceptable.

Short-answer and essay questions require the student to produce material, so are production questions. Just as with writing an assignment, short answer and essay questions need guiding criteria. These criteria include the following:

1. Write the criteria for grading the essay question into each question. Example (after writing a question about battles of the Civil War):

> For 12 points, include three specific battle dates, names of the corresponding three battles, and the names of the winning generals. Then describe the significance of one of the battles.

2. You may choose to put a rubric on the test that explains how the essay question will be graded. A rubric for a 20-point essay question follows.

Quality Indicators for Scoring

Criteria	4 Points	3 Points	2 Points	1 Point
1. Length	5 paragraphs	4 paragraphs	3 paragraphs	< 3 paragraphs
2. Grammar	0 errors	1 error	2 errors	3+ errors
3. Spelling	0 errors	1 error	2 errors	3+ errors
4. Content clearly addresses	4 issues	3 issues	2 issues	1 issue

3. At the beginning of the test, tell students in writing if points will be subtracted for grammar and spelling, and if so, how many points.

4. If a student says his or her handwriting is illegible and that they need to use a laptop to write the answers, this issue is probably handled by the college's accommodations center. At many colleges, students only get the accommodation if they request help from the accommodations center. Send students there first, at the very beginning of the semester. It can be very difficult for you to monitor what a student is reading on the laptop while taking the test. In the accommodations center, a trained specialist administers the test to the student, who probably writes on the computer in the office that has no Internet access or other files. It has been my experience that when a student asks for this accommodation and I reply that he or she may certainly go to the accommodations center for this service, the student does not. It makes me think that the individual wanted to use his or her laptop for cheating, not just writing.

Each college or university has its own version of the accommodations center. Some call it student support services or something similar. This is an office that coordinates accommodations for special education/special needs students, and most centers will only make accommodations available to those who have been diagnosed with a need and provide the supporting paperwork. Accommodations must be made early in the semester. When a student just arrives for an exam with the laptop and requests to use it, we cannot make that accommodation on a one-on-one basis.

Rules for Test Writing

1. Write the test before you teach the unit—not the night before. The test should be written to your objectives for teaching the material.
2. Make sure that the directions are clear for each section of the test.
3. Allow lots of space for students to write. Why? Research shows that clean, clear tests with more white space actually have higher scores than tests with little spaces for writing.
4. Explain the point values of the questions with each question.
5. Choose questions appropriate to the material.

Matching—for vocabulary or characters from a novel
Fill in the blank—when there is one clear answer
Yes/no or true/false—when much material needs to be quickly assessed
Short answer—when there is more than one right answer
Multiple choice—testing for facts and basic knowledge
Essay—when testing for in-depth answers that require students to support an argument

6. Time yourself taking the test. Allow twice that long for your students to take the test.

WHEN THE TEST IS DONE

1. Make a key for yourself. This is essential. Decide what the right answer is. Write it down. Grade one page at a time; for example, grade everybody's page 1, then page 2, then page 3.
2. Put the score on the test. You can explain the scale on the board, but it is generally not accepted to put scales on the board and then write how many students received each letter grade—for example, 6 As, 5 Bs, 7 Cs, 2 Ds, 2 Fs. Students will want to try to figure out who got the Fs, so this type of reporting may even break FERPA (Federal Education and Right to Privacy Act) regulations. The bell curve went out decades ago in education. Grade for mastery.
3. Never tell a student another student's grade or point out "Suzie got the highest grade." Never return tests in order of high to low or low to high; this practice is discriminatory. Do not have students distribute tests. Put them

in folders or distribute them yourself. Again, federal laws govern student privacy.

4. If students are allowed to keep their tests, they will share them with every friend, relative, and acquaintance. Keep them in folders in your locked file cabinet until well past the end of the semester. If you have enough space, keep fall exams until the end of the spring semester, and spring ones until the end of the next fall semester, just for your own accountability.

COMBATING CHEATING ON TESTS

Why do college students cheat? Many cheat because they feel such intense pressure to pass courses and have a low sense of self-esteem and accomplishment. They lack the confidence to take the test on their own, without the support of their plan for cheating. Some professors argue that we force students to cheat by not being clear about what to expect on a test, or by covering too much material, or by giving students too much to memorize. Making criterion-referenced exams that test what was taught, in a timely manner, will give students more confidence about taking tests. There is also nothing wrong with giving some practice tests, so that students know what is coming. To further prevent cheating, use these strategies:

1. Make students close all books and notebooks, and put them in their backpacks, and then those backpacks must be under their seats. Do not allow earphones, iPods, hats, or sunglasses.
2. Walk around the room as students take their tests, or stand in the back of the room where you can see everyone and they can't see where you are looking without turning around. This is called proctoring the exam, and it is a good way to monitor.
3. Tell students that their work must be their own or they will face the consequences of cheating outlined by the college, and tell them what these consequences are. Remind students of the college's policy on cheating every time they take an exam, and write it on the board and on a poster in the room. This policy should also be in your syllabus.
4. It is sometimes better for you to ask students to raise their hand when done so that you can pick up their test. Then they may leave.
5. Students should not be allowed to get a drink of water or use the restroom during a test. This provides them with an opportunity to go out into the hall, read answers that they have on a piece of paper in their pocket, and then return and write those answers on a test. With technology, they can use their cell phone to check the Internet or text a friend for answers. Asking to

leave the room is a trick as old as time itself. I bring a box of tissues into the classroom on exam days, so that sneezing is not an excuse to leave the room either. Again, tell students this and write it on the board.

6. Some professors seat students as they enter the room for the final, or give preassigned seats different than those where students would regularly sit. It's another precaution. Try to separate students as much as possible for maximum space between them.

CHAPTER 6

Methods of Teaching: Lectures, Graphic Organizers, and Concepts

Lectures

The lecture has been the standard teaching method in higher education for centuries—professors lecture and students listen. Why are lectures used? They are an effective way to convey a lot of material in a relatively short amount of time. A lecture can be given to hundreds, maybe even thousands, of students at one time. A lecture is a way for a subject matter expert to share his or her content knowledge quickly and succinctly. And yes, many students learn a lot from a well-prepared lecture.

Lecture has its place in teaching. Years ago professors actually started debating whether to lecture or teach with "student-centered" activity approaches. How absurd to think that our teaching should be one or the other! The term *constructivism* has worked its way from the K–12 classrooms to college teaching, and many colleges advocate constructive, hands-on teaching and learning. Activities and discovery learning have a place in college teaching and so does the lecture. The truth is that students cannot discuss the ramifications of a war until they know the facts about that war. They can't practice math problems until they have seen some solved. They can't develop a new marketing strategy as a project in their business class until they know what makes a successful marketing strategy. Having students work in pairs and in groups is useful, but we have to remember that they first have to be presented with new material in order to have something to practice and learn. Hence, lectures and presentations need to be made, and they need to be effective.

However, there are disadvantages in using too much teacher talk. Callahan, Clark, and Kellough (2002) remind instructors that they generally talk too much, talk too fast, and often are not even heard, much less understood. They write that "just because students have heard something before does not necessarily mean that they understood or have learned it" (p. 252).

To avoid the pitfalls of talking too much with little student understanding, lectures and presentations need to be well planned and executed. Tips include the following:

1. Be visual. At the very minimum, the main points of your lecture need to be projected onto the screen of the classroom. The notes that are projected must be large enough for all to read—even those students seated in the back. Fonts need to be 24 point or larger to be seen clearly on a screen. I used to prepare my notes and then make transparencies for the overhead projector. Now, with technology, I can create my notes, and show them directly from the computer in the rooms where I teach. I just carry a flash drive. Some professors rely on pulling up their notes from a system their campus has, but I prefer to not depend on the campus servers or Internet. Some professors create their 24-point size notes on paper and simply lay the paper on the Elmo big screen projector. Whatever is available—use it!

   Students deserve to see a skeletal outline of your talk. Also, using pre-prepared notes allows you to use spell-check and grammar-check programs so that you don't have to remember how to spell every word. Time is saved by not having to write on the board. What if you want to show a step-by-step procedure or solve a problem? Write the steps ahead of time and then put the first step up, then the next, and so forth. Time is still saved and you don't make a mistake while writing on a chalkboard/whiteboard. One last advantage of student notes on the screen is that you only have to prepare them once. You can update and improve on them with the simplest cut and paste. Also, a student can't say, "You never showed us that in class," because you have the exact notes you did show in class.

   Some professors put their skeletal notes online and tell students to print them out and bring them to class. Then, the students can really listen to the lecture and add in certain points. This also works well if you teach in a classroom/lecture hall that doesn't have technology. Others say that they refuse to put the notes online because they want the students to come to class and write and think during the lecture.

   Graphic organizers are a must in adding visuals to a lecture. They are so important that they are listed later in this chapter as a separate method.

2. Use the Internet and multimedia for even more visuals. The Internet provides wonderful resources for college instructors. Imagine lecturing about how cells reproduce and then showing a live clip from www.cellsalive.com, so that

students see cells reproducing. Teach about the Civil War and then show a reenactment from a DVD for 10 minutes. Introduce a lecture about Parker Palmer, or any author, by showing a five-minute YouTube video that the author made. Many of the books that I teach from in professional education courses have DVDs and companion websites with the authors discussing their own research and with scenes from out in the field. For example, my students might read about how to set up an ideal classroom for ninth graders, then I present the main points and then we watch a master high school teacher explain her classroom arrangement. Field trips are expensive—bringing the world into the classroom has become much more realistic.

3. Organize and break up the lecture. Charles C. Bonwell is noted for his work in the area of active learning in college classrooms. He contends that a lecture has the possibility to be interactive with the students, thereby making it "active learning" for them. Bonwell and Eison (1991) write about the modified lecture and suggest a structure of pauses, questions, and short student discussions within the lecture. Their ideas include pausing every 12 to 18 minutes, or even more frequently, and using the pause to have students talk with each other about the material. The students should answer questions, create new questions for the instructor, or review/check their factual notes (p. 10). Having students answer questions in these pauses with clickers, or other devices that allow instant feedback and tallying of responses, is a great way to make a lecture more interactive.

Skilled lecturers know that we are teaching a generation of young people who have grown up with myriad types of media and can have very short attention spans. I have heard it said that college students can pay attention only for the length of time a television show is on in between commercials. If that is true, then we must block our lectures into six- to eight-minute segments with some sort of "commercial break" in between where we make students write a question, solve a problem, or complete a step of a long procedure. Try this: Tell students to not write until you tell them to. Present new material for no more than 6 to 10 minutes, then say, "Now write the three most important points you have heard." Do you do this all the time? No, and it is critical that you use no one single method all the time, or even so much of the time that it becomes boring. Again, technology and clickers help us do this with large classes.

4. Use advance organizers. We all like to go to a presentation where the speaker catches our attention. An advance organizer can be as simple as a quote on the screen, or a question. It can be the two-minute YouTube video or a DVD clip. An advance organizer sets the stage and helps to make the connection for the learner. Additionally, an effective lecture has an introduction, a body,

and a conclusion. It is interesting, thought-provoking, and goes well above just pointing out what was written in the book.

5. Implement the New American Lecture. Silver, Strong, and Perini (2007) write about the New American Lecture, stating that in this type of lecture, the instructor provides the students with support to learn the material of the lecture. To develop and implement this type of lecture, the instructor should

   a. connect the learner to past knowledge and build new connections, designing an activity that hooks students into the content and links students' initial ideas to the content to come.
   b. provide the students with a visual organizer that lays out the structure of the lecture content.
   c. use memory devices and active participation techniques.
   d. conduct periodic thinking reviews.
   e. provide synthesis and reflection activities. (p. 21)

6. Use your voice and prepare the delivery of the lecture. While it almost goes without saying, it does have to be said that instructors who lecture must have clear speaking voices that can be heard throughout the classroom/lecture hall. Use a microphone if needed. Vary the tone of voice. Don't scream at students, but also don't mumble or whisper. And yes, when you are new at delivering lectures, you should practice them aloud in front of a mirror. In addition to projecting the large-font notes on the screen, put those notes in front of you and add the other points you want to make. Use red pens or highlighters. If you plan to walk around, use a clipboard to carry your notes. Make eye contact with students. Look at students and watch for their reactions. If you are teaching in a 75-minute block of time, have students stand and stretch (while discussing an answer to a question, of course) and then sit back down. Have a pleasant bell or timer to quiet students after these one- to two-minute mini-discussions and to let them know that their conversation is over and the lecture has resumed.

Graphic Organizers

If a picture is truly worth a thousand words, then a graphic organizer is worth even more, as it combines words and pictures to help students organize concepts and information.

The KWL chart is a tool for introducing new material, assessing students' prior knowledge, finding out what students want to learn about the subject,

and then reviewing. The K is for knowledge (what they think they know), the W is for want to learn, and the L is for learned (review). By the time students get to college, they may already know a lot about a subject, or they may have some false assumptions. Students can write what they know at their seats, on chart paper around the room, on the whiteboard, or with the use of clickers and texting depending on the size of your room and what is available. Then, the effective teacher takes what students have written and fills in the blanks, so to speak. History instructors can find this very effective, as they ask students what they know about the Vietnam and Iraq wars. Political science professors find students have many false assumptions about government and its workings. Finding out what students know and where they got that information is an important lesson for us as well. Once we know these things, we can work toward undoing false assumptions and teach the students how to be better interpreters of information.

Having students write what they learned is a good review activity. If you want to assess informally what students have learned, have them turn in the L section of the KWL chart just so you can read it and see if they understand the material clearly. You may want to give some points for turning in class work like this, as it then becomes an objective form of giving participation points. Students who were there and have three sentences written on their "what I learned" section get three points. It's an idea, and as a new college instructor, you need to experiment with new ideas and find the ones that work best for you in the classes that you teach. Obviously, some freshmen classes need more incentives to be in class and be taking notes than some upperclassmen. I know some professors of graduate classes who use participation points. Good, effective teaching takes place when the instructor finds what works with the population of students in their institution—and those populations are changing annually in many of our institutions.

KWL CHART

Topic _____

What I know	What I want to know	What I learned
1.	1.	1.
2.	2.	2.
3.	3.	3.
4.	4.	4.
5.	5.	5.

WEBBING

Webbing can be a good graphic organizer when the instructor is trying to relate characters in a novel, ancillary ideas to the big idea, or just about any topic. The web is like an outline, but for students who need to see a big, global picture before they can understand the details of whatever is being studied. The web shown here (figure 6.1) is actually for a very famous American novel. Any guesses? Yes, it was designed for use when teaching *Gone with the Wind* by Margaret Mitchell. Does it help you think about characters? Plot? If you haven't read the book, are you now interested in doing so? What could you use a web for in your subject area? Would you project it onto the screen? Would you give students a blank web and have them fill in the circles? Would you have students brainstorm an original web with a partner for a few minutes, then have one or two groups show and describe their webs of what they read the night before? As with many of the graphic organizers, webs help you introduce, explain, or review material. The webs can help students visualize the material, and then build their knowledge.

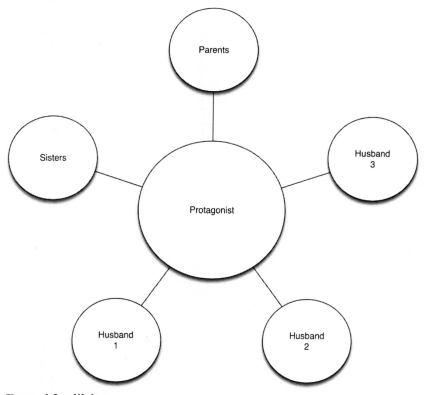

Figure 6.1.   Web

FLOWCHARTS

Long-used by computer programmers, flowcharts (see figure 6.2) can help all students get organized, and like it or not, as college professors we are now charged with helping students learn how to learn and how to organize their notes and materials. Having students make a flowchart of how to think out the steps of a problem or how to write a long paper can really help them. Many students are overwhelmed when given a large assignment of any kind, and flowcharting the steps will help them see how to start—and complete—the assignment. When presented with this idea, some professors say, "But that's what high school was for." While we all hope that students did learn these skills in high school, our experiences with students often show us that they didn't. Providing graphic organizers should help students who weren't challenged in high school with large projects, or who got through high school doing the minimum.

Figure 6.2. Flowchart

THE CYCLE GRAPH

The cycle graph (see figure 6.3) is another way to help students organize their thinking and learning. What ideas do you have that would work for this graphic in your class?

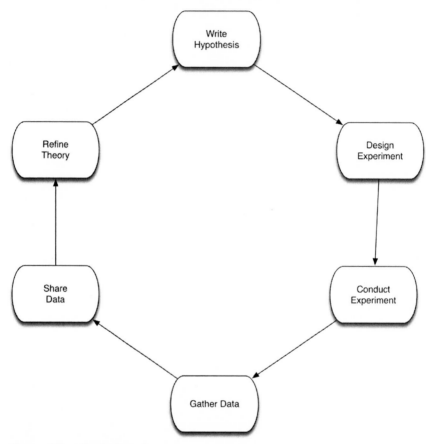

Figure 6.3.   Cycle Graph

THE VENN DIAGRAM

Venn diagrams (see figure 6.4) are used so frequently that even third graders should recognize them. Why should we bring them into college-level classes? At the college level, we are striving to teach higher-order thinking skills and to teach students to discern concepts and traits at a much deeper level than they have been exposed to in previous schooling. The Venn diagram gets us started, serves as an advance organizer, or lets us review what we have said in a lecture. Most importantly, it helps students organize and sort material, which is so critical for learning.

All of the graphic organizers we use help students to learn the basics, which then enables them to learn the more complex issues as a result. If learning is like building a house, the graphics are the foundation, and then the house can be built.

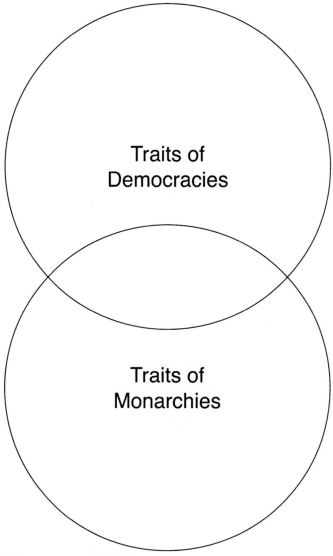

Figure 6.4. Venn Diagram

Concept Attainment

An integral part of teaching any subject is the teaching of concepts. A concept is an idea, a thought, an abstraction, or a view. What are some of the key concepts in your field? Do they include light, matter, gravity, and propulsion? Are they democracy, communism, monarchy, and socialism? Eggen and Kauchak (2006) write, "The concept attainment model is an inductive teaching strategy designed to help students of all ages reinforce their understanding of concepts and practice hypothesis testing" (p. 167). According to these authors, a lesson can be developed by presenting students with examples and non-examples of the concept and having students hypothesize possible names of concepts based on the examples. After the hypothesis step, instructors then have students analyze additional examples until a single hypothesis is isolated and defined (Eggen & Kauchak, 2006, p. 184). This inductive model is sometimes called discovery teaching and is often used by instructors who include it as part of their active learning classes.

Other authors contend that concepts can be taught deductively as well as inductively.

> Deductive teaching is defined as a style of teaching in which the instructor presents the class with one or more concepts or principles, challenges students to investigate a set of examples that are related to these main ideas, and then asks the students to test or apply the central ideas. (Gabler & Schroeder, 2003, p. 122)

The key to teaching concepts is to decide how to present. Will it be easier and quicker to teach the basics deductively? Will there be times that you want to lead your students through a process where they come up with the rules or criteria that define the concepts? Will using both ways work well throughout the semester? Some students want to learn deductively. They want a clear path to knowing what the concept means. Other students truly want to figure things out for themselves and seem to remember things longer and have a deeper understanding if they approach learning inductively. Disassembling and reassembling abstract concepts, as well as things, helps students learn, and discovering the concept may hold the interest of some students. Use both approaches to teach concepts and to keep students thinking. See the template for planning a concept attainment lesson for more suggestions.

PLANNING A CONCEPT ATTAINMENT LESSON

Think of 10 commonly taught concepts in your field. While commonly taught, they should also be higher order concepts that need more than a few minutes to teach.

1. List the most challenging of the 10 concepts to teach.

2. Define this concept.

3. List three to five vocabulary words associated with this concept that should be taught simultaneously.

4. List three basic characteristics of this concept.

Examples of this concept include

1.

2.

3.

Non-examples of this concept include

1.

2.

3.

This concept is important because . . .

This concept is tied to previous learning through . . .

Conclusion

The one thing that all college instructors agree on is that there is much subject content to teach our students. It is the how to teach the content where disagreement begins. How we teach is dependent on many factors—what the content is, how much time we have to teach it, who the students are, and yes, even who we are. I can teach quite a bit through role-play activities in teacher education classes, but that teaching method is probably of very little use in a physics class. As a learner, I know that I need to see the material, not just hear it, so I always have visuals in my lectures. As we teach in all levels of colleges and universities, we need to think critically about how we teach, choosing when to lecture, when to add visuals, and how to teach the important concepts of our disciplines. Once we have imparted information, then it's time to get the students to use the information, and the next chapters deal with guiding students to talk, think, and produce quality work.

CHAPTER 7

Methods for Teaching with Active Learning: Questions, Discussions, and Group Work

Have you ever heard a colleague say, "Well, I taught it, but they didn't learn it"? Have you been surprised when a concept you thought was covered completely in your class, was missed by multiple students on the exam? Have you ever felt that your students were asleep or brain dead, because there is no other explanation for their performance? Much research has been done about the learning process, and some of the results indicate that "students are simply more likely to internalize, understand, and remember material learned through active engagement in the learning process" (Bonwell & Sutherland, 1996, p. 3). Just what is meant by *active learning* or *active engagement*? And is this the same as learner-centered or student-centered instruction?

All three phrases—active learning, learner-centered instruction, and student-centered instruction—can have different connotations depending on the writer. All three phrases have been used by some instructors to indicate that they are doing more than lecturing and giving exams. Considered a leader in the field of learner-centered teaching in higher education, Maryellen Weimer (2002) writes,

> It is not possible to sample even a modest amount of the literature on learning and continue teaching as most of us were taught. Very little there justifies traditional approaches, especially given the learning need of students and society today. At some level, most of us already know this. We have embraced the methods of active learning, cooperative and collaborative learning, and writing across the curriculum, to name but a few of the initiatives, that put students in new relationships with content, their fellow learners, and their teachers. (pp. 19–20)

Responding to questions, participating in discussions, and group work are three common examples of active learning, as they require students to do something. While not new methods in education, they are methods that can enhance teaching and learning, and are often quite "doable" in the college classroom.

Teaching with Questions

Certainly not new, teaching with questions—getting the students to think—is a technique even Socrates used. To improve upon our teaching, we need to look at the kinds of questions we ask, how we can get students to answer higher-order questions, and how to deliver our questions.

KINDS OF QUESTIONS

1. Questions to Assess Prior Interest and Knowledge

When we start a new unit or topic within our courses, we should determine what the students already know about the material. If we discover that they know a lot of the basics, we can move forward quickly. If they do not know the background information, we may have to back up and spend time building necessary prerequisite knowledge.

How do we assess prior interest and knowledge? Not with yes/no questions. Our students may tell us that they know in order to not look dumb, but in reality they don't know the material. We have to ask open-ended questions that we can assess. We have to make students do some problems. We have to have students demonstrate. Coaches know this well. They don't ask star players if they can shoot the ball through the hoop. They take the player to the court and watch him shoot the ball.

Sometimes we ask these pre-assessment questions at the beginning of the course on the interest inventory or a pretest. Other times we ask them as we start individual lessons. Remember that students often have wrong information and that we have to find out their misconceptions as well as their correct ones in order to teach them.

In small classes (25 students and under), the teacher can probably lead the discussion by asking questions and calling on individuals. For larger groups, you may have to divide students into pairs or small groups, ask questions, and then get responses. If you must divide into groups, also find a way to determine if all or only some of the students know the answers. Following is one way to do this:

1. Divide students into groups.
2. Provide a handout or show the following on the screen:
   - Write your group's answer to the questions.
   - Was this answer confirmed as correct by the lecture that followed?
   - Record how many in your group would have given this answer on their own (4/5; 2/3; 3/3).
3. Collect these at the end of the lesson or at the end of the assessment question piece. They can be anonymous. This is not evaluation of students' knowledge. It is formative assessment to help you teach the topic.

Personal response devices, such as clickers, make pre-assessment easy in large classes, as the professor asks a question, students touch the response, and totals appear on the screen for the class. Some professors require students to answer pre-assessment questions online before class. The responses show the professor where to allocate time in the presentation. Pre-assessments are not graded on right/wrong answers, but you may want to assign participation points for completing the online assignment.

2. Convergent Questions

As teachers, we often give many convergent questions, as these questions lead students to one answer. Convergent questions are excellent discussion starters, too. In my teacher education classes, I might ask students to count up the number of teachers that they remember from their elementary school experiences. After doing so, I would ask, how many of you have more women than men on this list? Why is this typical? Why do more women become elementary teachers than men? What are some possible reasons?

By introducing the topic of women in education in this manner, students will probably remember the reasons better than if I were to just start my lecture by stating that over 75 percent of all teachers in K–12 schools are women. By asking convergent questions about women in education, I have found a great introduction to my lecture about K–12 teaching being the family-friendly profession.

In other fields of study, convergent questions might include the following:

What is the main theme of the essay?
What do you see in the novel that is straight from the author's own life?

After doing an experiment, ask students what they saw happen and direct them to the correct reasons for what they saw.

3. Divergent Questions

Sometimes we want students to think about questions that have many answers. We want students to think broadly and to become problem solvers for complex problems. To get students to practice this, we ask them divergent questions. For example (and for heated debate by any group of college students):

How could your college experience be improved?
How could your major be improved?
How could campus housing be improved?

If there are no right and wrong answers to some divergent questions, why are we asking them? We ask them to stimulate discussion, to brainstorm research ideas, or to provide ideas for writing prompts. In some areas, such as science, we ask the divergent questions to stimulate discussion of ethical issues and "hot topics." We ask divergent questions because there are no simple answers to some questions. Examples:

How could the United States have avoided the Iraq war that began in 2003?
   How can we avoid future ones in the Middle East?
How could the United States have avoided skyrocketing gas prices after 2007?
   What can be done now to lesson oil dependency?

4. Focus Questions

Focus questions ask students to think about material in a certain way with a given focus. For example, in a teacher education class, I give my students some factual information and then question them to focus on the meaning of the information. Example: In 2008, most teachers in public K–12 schools made $40,000 to $80,000 a year. Some teachers had higher salaries. Administrators' salaries generally started at $80,000 and higher. My questions to focus students on teacher salaries are as follows:

Why is this good news?
Why is it bad news?
How much does a house cost, on average? A car?
What should teachers look at besides salary when interviewing for a job?

In a literature class, focus questions direct students to understand plot and characters. In a history class, focus questions help students understand the whys behind the facts and figures.

5. Evaluative Questions

Evaluative questions force students to form an opinion. As college instructors we need to teach students to read, research, and debate answers in order to develop educated opinions. Evaluative questions are higher-order questions and are not easily answered. They should force students to learn to organize their thoughts, while also applying the skills of logic.

Examples:

Should the United States drill for all off-shore oil possible?
Should Louisiana allow people to rebuild in the hurricane zones?
Should there be term limits in the U.S. Senate and House?

At the college level, students have long been known to want to debate and argue every conceivable issue. This is, in part, why higher education exists—to provide the venue for deep thought, for both professors and students. However, we have to be careful to ask questions and guide discussions in a manner that does not offend students and that does not allow for the possibility of students offending other students. With evaluative questions, the possibilities are open for student misuse and offense. We have to know that we are responsible and accountable for student learning and for their protection from bullying and offensive language in our courses.

HIGHER ORDER QUESTIONS

In 1956, Benjamin Bloom and a group of other researchers developed a taxonomy of objectives regarding the thinking and reasoning abilities of students (see, for example, Moore, 2005). Known simply as Bloom's Taxonomy, it is used by K–12 teachers throughout the United States for writing both lesson objectives and questions. The six categories of this taxonomy are knowledge, comprehension, application, analysis, synthesis, and evaluation. The taxonomy is listed in order, with lower-order thinking skills at the bottom, and higher ones at the top. It is very helpful to know about Bloom's Taxonomy as you write objectives for your classes and as you write questions for discussion and testing purposes.

How can using the taxonomy help you with teaching and help students to learn? First of all, think about what you want students to know and be able to do by the end of individual lessons and by the end of your course. Most professors relate that they want students to be able to apply their learning, to analyze problems, to synthesize material, and to evaluate materials and solutions. These outcomes are higher-order thinking skills. If, however, we only ask students to identify answers at the knowledge and comprehension levels (lower-order thinking skills) in our daily classes, they will not be able to apply, analyze, synthesize, or evaluate on the final exam or in life. So, we must get students to think and answer questions at the higher levels every day in class. To do this, it helps to see action verbs associated with each level of the taxonomy.

Level	Action Verbs
Knowledge	identify, define, list, match, state, name, label, describe, select
Comprehension	translate, convert, generalize, paraphrase, rewrite, summarize, distinguish, infer, alter, explain
Application	use, operate, produce change, solve, show, compute, prepare, determine
Analysis	discriminate, select, distinguish, separate, subdivide, identify, break down, analyze, compare
Synthesis	design, plan, compile, compose, organize, conclude, arrange, construct, devise
Evaluation	appraise, compare, justify, criticize, explain, interpret, conclude, summarize, evaluate (Moore, 2005, p. 92)

As you write questions for class discussion, keep this list in front of you. Use the action verbs. Then, as you write the exam questions, use the same action verbs for those questions. Student achievement tends to go up as students are asked to answer questions that mirror the cognitive levels at which they were taught and which they practiced in class. As a further example, a calculus professor asked me why I thought so many of his students sat in class, looked like they understood, but then failed the exams. I began my answer by explaining Bloom's Taxonomy. "At which levels do your students participate in class?" I asked.

He replied, "They watch me demonstrate problems in class, and my questions are about the next steps, etc., so I guess that's knowledge and comprehension."

"That sounds right, and very typical. Now, how do you test them?"

"Well, on the exams I want them to show me that they can apply what they have learned. They have to analyze a problem, and evaluate which way to best solve problems, then do them. I make the problems much tougher than any seen in class or homework."

"Well, if you want students to apply, analyze, and evaluate on the exams, they better start practicing those skills in every class. Instead of you solving every problem, model some, then have groups of students solve the tougher ones. Literally make them a visual flowchart of how they have to think about these problems in order to do them. If they spend parts of each class doing the higher-order thinking, then, and maybe only then, will they be able to do it on a test—and beyond. We want them to know these math skills so well that they can apply them to engineering problems in real life, right?"

This conversation could have been with an instructor of any subject area. If we want the students to achieve at higher-order thinking skills, then we have to include those in our questioning on a daily level. Most importantly, we have to align how we test to how we have taught.

PRACTICE WITH
BLOOM'S TAXONOMY

Choose a topic/activity for your field _____

Now, for each level of the taxonomy, write a question that fits the topic. Your questions will build form lower-order thinking skills (knowledge) to higher-level ones (evaluation).

1. Knowledge

2. Comprehension

3. Application

4. Analysis

5. Synthesis

6. Evaluation

DELIVERY OF QUESTIONS

Now that you know that there are many types of questions and that questions are asked at different levels of cognition, it's time to think about how to deliver questions for maximum effectiveness. Think about your own college experiences. Were you ever in a class where a few students dominated? Or in a class where you wanted to hide? Were you ever in a class where you answered a question to the best of your ability, and then the professor laughed or, worse yet, made fun of you and had another student give the right answer? To avoid these poor approaches, let's look at some question and answer guidelines.

1. Think about why you are asking the questions in the first place. If it is to assess student knowledge and understanding of an assignment, then you may need a way to get a variety of students to answer, not just the prepared students and show-offs who always know. When you ask any question, decide *beforehand* if you are willing to let anyone call out the answer, or if you want to call on someone. Then, and this is vitally important—let the students know what you want. You can develop a style of asking questions and letting anyone call out by simply starting out that way and letting your body posture and nonverbal expressions indicate that anyone can answer. Or you can be explicit and say, "Anyone can answer."

To ensure that students do not call out answers, you need to tell students that you are giving them 15 seconds of think time, and then you will call on someone. You may give the think time and then ask for hands of volunteers. To lower stress, ask a tough question, tell students to tell their answer to a partner, and then ask for volunteers to share answers. Some researchers in this field say to "ask your well-worded question before calling on a student for a response" (Callahan, Clark, & Kellough, 2002, p. 270).

I once saw a very sly young instructor tell his class that he had put their names in a bag, and students would be called upon randomly to answer the questions. He did have a bag with their names, and he occasionally called on the person whose name was picked, but honestly, he sometimes called on someone else who he wanted to answer and made the students just think it was all random. This is a clever delivery of questions to get all students involved, which was his goal for that day's class.

Of course, all of these suggestions can be useful in delivering questions. The key is to have variety and to decide when to do each type of delivery.

2. Once students answer questions, then what? Students deserve professional feedback that helps them to learn. We do not laugh at student answers. We do not demean student answers. We do not ridicule. We provide feedback in a professional manner that allows the student to learn if his or her answer is correct. We all learn by feedback.

The best hint for giving feedback is to remember that you are assumed to be the expert in the room. If student A gives an incorrect answer, *you* should answer the question, not another student. This doesn't hurt the esteem of the student, as you should know the answer, while having another student give the corrections can be humiliating. If a question is a multipart one, then one student can start an answer, and another add the next step.

3. What about praise?   There is research that says that praising a student may actually cause him or her to quit trying as hard and to have less intrinsic motivation. It's like giving the child a piece of candy for every correct behavior. On the other hand, do you like to know if an answer is appropriate and do you like to occasionally hear an emphatic "yes" or "absolutely right"? I think we all do. We just have to be careful with praise. Praise is about the answer or the student behavior, not about the student's inherent goodness or intelligence.

And we do not ever use phrases like, "Yes, just like my most brilliant foreign graduate students would answer," or "Not bad for a female," or "Not bad for a football player." If you want to lose your job quickly or get sued or both, those responses might just do it. They cannot ever be used, even in joking—and you shouldn't be thinking them, either.

The best advice on praise is to provide the feedback about a right or wrong answer, then use praise in private. Praise may be less controversial and more appropriate when written on a student's paper or given in a private conference. We have to be very careful of every word we say in the classroom, and that includes praise. On the other hand, many students have a strong need for praise and for the reinforcement that it can convey. Discuss this with other instructors in your department and college.

4. Allow enough wait time.   It has been said that if instructors wait long enough, someone will answer. I am always surprised that we expect answers immediately, even to higher-order questions. We should allow wait time for students to think. How many times do we hear answers with little or no thought behind them? Well, it takes time to think. We should build in wait time, never calling on anyone for 8 to 10 seconds, so that all can think about potential answers. We should tell students about wait time, and build it in to our questioning skills.

5. Students answer our class questions when they feel that the class is a safe environment in which to speak.   Many of our students have fragile egos, and they certainly do not want to be embarrassed publicly in front of their peers. We need to remember to always be humane when asking questions and when responding to answers. No student will learn from questions that simply scare them to death or from responses that humiliate them. We need to be nice. We need to be professional. We need to be polite, yet assertive. Sarcasm is not acceptable.

Group Discussions

College professors often lament that students simply will not participate in discussions. When our students do not participate in discussions, we need to ask ourselves the following questions:

1. What was the purpose of the discussion? (to generate ideas for future research? to prove mastery of the readings? to have students think of original solutions to difficult questions?)
2. What were the students supposed to do? In other words, what was the objective of the discussion? Just as for any lesson, we should be able to write, "By the end of the discussion, the student will be able to . . ."
3. Was the classroom climate appropriate for a discussion? Did students know one another well enough to discuss a topic in a full-group setting? Were there student incivility issues that might limit a discussion?
4. Had the students been taught routines for the discussion part of class? Did they literally know "how to discuss"?
5. How did you plan to use the material discussed in later classes? Or, how were students to use the material discussed in later classes?

Several conditions must exist for classroom discussions to work. There must be a reason for the discussion, and the discussion should have an objective that fits into the curriculum. Certain classroom procedures and routines must be introduced before large-group discussions so that students know how to discuss, and students need to feel a level of trust exists between teacher and student and among students. What kinds of routines need to be in place? Baldwin, Keating, and Bachman (2006) suggest, "You might want to begin with mini-groups of six to eight students clustered for discussion before moving to whole-class discussions" (p. 96). You need to get to know your students before starting discussions. If an instructor knows that some students will dominate, or actually take over, he or she needs to bring in a timer and limit comments to a number of seconds.

If there is to be true discussion, students need to see each other, so room arrangements matter. Other tips for facilitating successful discussion include the following:

1. Remind students of basic ground rules—like active listening, when to not interrupt, and respect of everyone else's time and opinion.
2. Select appropriate questions to start and guide the discussion. Ask yourself, is the purpose of this discussion divergent, convergent, or evaluative in nature?
3. Let students respond to each other, or it's not a discussion; it's teacher-led questioning.

Why have discussions? Discussions are a great way to preview and review material. They create a venue for students to ask questions of each other, not just the instructor. Discussions do help students understand material. Asking students to discuss their thought processes when solving last night's math problems not only provides answers to the problems, but also lets the instructor know where students may be having trouble with new concepts.

Fill in the discussion planning sheet template before your next class discussion.

PLANNING FOR A MEANINGFUL WHOLE-CLASS DISCUSSION

Topic: _____

This discussion is to (circle one or more that apply) preview material, generate interest, focus students, get students to see one point, get students to see many points, review material, explain material, or other _____ .
Points written on board for students:

1. By the end of this discussion you will be able to . . .

2. During the discussion, you will be expected to . . .

3. You will use the material/topic/ideas of this discussion as you . . . (this relates the discussion to a paper to be written or to a test or an essay)

Teacher questions to start the discussion:

1.

2.

3.

Review of routine for how to conduct a discussion:

1. Only one person may speak at a time, directing statements at others.

2. Respect all opinions given.

3. Review this routine or post on the board *before* starting the discussion.

Group Work

Group work encompasses many things and has many names. Some instructors use the name *cooperative group work* and follow strict guidelines for that style of group work. Others use group work informally. For decades, college students were taught to do their own work, to problem solve alone, and to never get help for an outside assignment. That approach has changed dramatically, and now professors often require that projects be done by a group, or that students have peer edits of papers and assignments. To support the use of group work, Silver, Strong, and Perini (2007) write,

> Students who are well-versed in the skills of cooperative learn-ing—skills like active listening, effective communication, consensus building, and conflict resolution—are better able to solve challenging problems, formulate clear and cogent opinions, and produce first-rate work. Moreover, as the workforce of the future, students who can understand and work effectively with their peers hold a signifi-cant advantage over students whose academic life is marked largely by independent seatwork. (p. 183)

Group work is successful when advance planning takes place.

1. Students are divided into groups for each specific activity. No students should be put into a group for a whole semester, or even several weeks. Care needs to be taken to divide students according to the task. Yes, for some short activities students can self-select into groups of three to five. For other activities, you may want to sort the students into groups based on what you see as students' strengths. Groups should be heterogeneous, as groupings such as males versus females were deemed poor practice in teaching decades ago. If students are allowed to choose their own groups, foreign students, or other groups, may all choose to work together, and self-selected segregation does not help to foster a collegial classroom. Callahan, Clark, and Kellough (2002) base their summary of cooperative groupings on the pioneering work of Slavin, and write that

> the theory of cooperative learning is that when small groups of students of mixed backgrounds and capabilities work together toward a com-mon goal, members of the group increase their friendship and respect for one another. As a consequence, each individual's self-esteem is enhanced, students are more motivated to participate in higher-order thinking, and academic achievement is accomplished. (p. 227)

Anytime we ask students to work together, we must be aware of their mis-givings about the process of collaborating. Some students will simply refuse to participate or will refuse to be in a certain group. By allowing them to join a different group or sit out one activity as a listener, we are respecting them. Becoming authoritative or combative will not help the situation. However, even those who only listen are accountable for the material being studied. Be aware that some students will read a syllabus, and upon discovering that many group projects are required or that group work is graded, will try to drop your class and take someone else's. By reading the rest of the guidelines presented here, these pitfalls to group work can be avoided.

   2. Time frames must be stated and followed, and be generally short.   Group work can often be most successful if it is used for less than one class period. Longer project group work becomes difficult. Today's students have such busy schedules that it is not feasible to meet and study together or to plan their group's presentation together. If they have to work together, the instructor has to budget the time for all the work. Students may work in a group, decide who does what outside of class, and then finish the work in another class, but be aware that there will be students who do nothing outside of class, or who do not return to class for the follow-up. Some professors contend that the group should be penalized when this happens. However, many educators now work on the premise that group work is *not* graded, but rather is the starting block for brainstorming or for review sessions and so forth (Kagan, 1995). A key to successful group work is to keep the time short and to have all the work done in class. Penalizing one student for another student's absence or lack of participation is a quick way to have complaints to the department chair, dean, and provost.

   3. Once the groupings are established and time frames determined, the next key is clear expectations of the goals of the group work.   Why are students in groups for the class and what is to be accomplished? Clarify the goals and objectives. For example, write out the objectives, stating that by the end of the group work session, each student will have two ideas for the next assignment and will have practiced writing an introductory paragraph.

   Another example: In my curriculum classes, students learn about curriculum mapping, a way to chart how to cover material in a given time frame by listing topics, objectives, learning experiences, and assessments. After much presentation of how to map curriculum, I divide students into groups of four or five, give each group poster paper and a pen, and then announce, "I want you to pick one content area and one specific unit topic. On one and only one sheet of paper, write a map for that topic for one week, with three smaller topics, three objectives, three learning experiences, and three sample assessments. Write the way you will be writing on your personal assignment. In about 20 minutes, you will present your group's map, explain it briefly, and I will give feedback that will give you an idea about how your individual papers will be graded." Of course, there is a visual outlining this on the screen, too.

Students work together, answering each other's questions and doing the thinking they should do before starting their individual assignments. Students listen to each other's presentations and to my feedback because I make comments like, "Wow, I would give this part of the assignment full credit because . . ." or "This is a good start on the assessment piece, but to earn full points, you would need to add x, y, and z, on your personal assignments." Students quickly learn that working in the group is very important. They don't want to miss class because they know our group work helps them get better grades on their assignments. And no one is graded on the group work. Its value is formative in nature, not summative for a grade.

4. Group work must be monitored.   In fact, another value of group work is the time it provides for the professor to individualize instruction. A student who is hesitant to ask a question aloud in a whole-group format is usually not hesitant at all to ask the professor as he or she moves around the room to assist groups by answering questions. Our presence in the room keeps students on track, and without our presence, even graduate students will get off task. A former colleague of mine assigned group work and left the room. Not only did this not help students learn, but her course evaluations were terrible.

Another way to monitor group work is to assign roles. Common roles for group participants include

1. the group facilitator (leader).
2. the recorder (person writes what the group will report back).
3. the reporter (person who reports back, but with the recorder's notes).
4. the timekeeper (watches time, but the leader leads).
5. the thinking monitor (different role depending on group work). This person may be used to find quotes from the readings, look up definitions of words, or watch the group process and report back on how the group could have been more efficient at the end of the session. (See, for example, Callahan, Clark, & Kellough, 2002, pp. 227–229, for more ideas for participants' roles.)

Key summary points for making group work successful:

1. Take care in the formation of groups—and keep the time frame for group work short.
2. Have a reason for group work and make the objectives clear.
3. Assign roles and monitor groups.
4. While groups need to present back to the class for feedback, grade only individuals' work. It is not fair to grade a student based on another student's participation or work. (For more on not grading group work, see Kagan, 1995.)

5. Don't use group work every day or even every week. Use it when it fits a goal for your teaching and student learning. I tend to use more teacher presentations and direct teaching early in the semester, and more group work at the end of the semester. After all, until my students learn the material, what would the have to discuss?

Uses of group work:

1. Brainstorming. Students need help deciding where to start on some assignments. The use of group work to brainstorm ideas can be time well spent. Have groups get together and brainstorm ideas for papers, experiments, and so on, and then have students break up and write on their own. Make assignments clear so that students know they can brainstorm together, but that they each write their own paper. There is no such thing as being too clear.
2. Problem solving. This application for college classes works well in most subject areas. Imagine groups of three solving a tough math problem, then explaining at the front of the class (with their visual). Ask social studies/history students to solve tough issue problems in small groups of three to five, then to present their solution with at least two direct quotes from the assigned reading. Working in small groups allows students time to talk amongst themselves, which is important in a large class setting.
3. Role-plays. While the goal of college teaching is optimal learning by the student, fun can be had. Role-plays can be a learning experience, and can be fun, too. Imagine acting out the roles of book characters with what they might have said to change the plot. Students can role-play being a presidential candidate or a senator during a time in history. Foreign language classes use role-playing a lot, as students can be waiters and customers in cafés, or customs agents at the airport. Can physics instructors use role-plays? Maybe or maybe not. Every method does not work with every subject.

The effective teacher selects the right teaching strategy for each lesson, based on the students, their backgrounds, the material to be covered, and the instructor's own comfort levels with teaching in certain ways. Group work is one way to get students to interact with the material. Grouping students for discussions, reviews, and brainstorming or problem-solving activities can be quite effective. As with any strategy or method, the true key for success is matching the goals of the lesson to the method that helps students learn.

GROUP WORK PLANNING GUIDE

1. Topic, goal, and objectives: Write out the question/problem(s) to be posed to the groups. Will you state the problem or do you need to create steps and give each group specific directions on a card?

Key: Why are we doing this in groups and not as individuals or as a whole class?

2. How many in each group? Why?

3. How long for each step of the group work? Why?

4. Accountability: What will the group do at the end of their work? How will individuals be held accountable? Will some individual work be graded as a group?

5. What special resources are needed to make this group work activity successful? (Props, paper, markers, timer, etc.)

CHAPTER 8

Online, Blended, and Technology-Enhanced Teaching

In the early 1990s, I attended a workshop on distance learning. The presenter said that distance learning made a weak instructor look even worse to the students in the class, and a strong instructor even better. His rationale was that weak instructors are disorganized, unclear, and generally not successful at engaging students in a regular classroom, and when they begin teaching via a camera to off-site classrooms, all of these weaknesses are magnified. On the other hand, a strong instructor would realize that he or she had to do everything that was already in place in the regular classroom, and then go beyond the basics to get students involved and learning in the satellite classrooms. A strong instructor should realize that this kind of teaching would be different and would require some study, practice, and change. This presenter's theory might still apply today to the many ways that we deliver online and blended courses with advanced technology.

Why Online?

The first reason for online college classes is that there are simply too many students entering higher education to be accommodated by traditional offerings. As record numbers of students start college, there are not enough seats available in classes.

The next reason is that students, and their expectations, have changed. We all know some students who do not want to attend 8 A.M. classes or classes at other times that they deem inconvenient. This is the "I want it my way" generation. So, they sleep late, hit a few classes, work at the 30-hour-a-week job, and then attend class online at a time when it is convenient—between midnight and 3 A.M. The idea that a discussion can be online, like texting their friends, appeals to some students. While this example is a bit stereotypic, today's students do want a lot of flexibility, and watching the professor's lecture from their apartment at 2 A.M. appeals to many students.

There are advertisements on billboards and on television for college degrees for "busy adults" and "working professionals." These ads show mothers with young children at a computer, or people in business suits at their laptops. These nontraditional learners might not have considered advanced degrees a few decades ago. No matter the stereotypes, online, blended, and technology-enhanced teaching meets the needs of hyper-busy traditional-aged students and adult learners. It is a way to get a degree without spending the traditional amounts of time, at the traditional hours, on campus. It reduces distance and time.

There are many ways to deliver classes with technology. Some universities still use distance learning the way I was introduced to it in the 1990s—a professor delivers class at a certain time in a specific site, and students at satellite sites receive the class via video or the Internet. There is a picture with audio, and it's interactive. The advantage is that one professor may serve more students and that students in geographically isolated areas can attend without driving to a main campus. E-mail or chat groups have enhanced this type of distance learning. The satellite sites may have a coordinator or teaching assistant who attends each session and delivers and proctors exams, or the exams may be online.

There are online programs where the student never meets the professors in person. Everything from readings to discussions is done online. Students may or may not need to be online at the same time (asynchronous). Sometimes students purchase their textbooks to supplement the online course, but not always. At some institutions, the entire degree is earned this way. Some highly respected universities, including Ivy League ones, are offering courses and degrees this way, especially at the graduate level.

Blended courses seem quite popular. While there are multiple definitions of blended, the students generally meet on campus for a certain number of hours, and then complete readings on their own, using technology for discussion groups and for mailing in assignments. The students may return to campus for a final group discussion and/or to take a final exam. I met an algebra professor who said that she didn't believe blended learning would work until she was assigned to teach this way. She brought the students in for a few class sessions, a midterm, and a final. She said that her grade distributions were the same as the on-campus classes. While she related this story to me informally at a conference, I hope she reflects and does some research about her successful teaching, then shares that with others learning to teach blended classes.

Communicating with Technology

Even if you are not teaching some version of an online course, you are probably using more technology than you realize to communicate with students. Why? Because students expect and demand it!

E-mail, Facebook, Twitter, Ning, blogs, wikis, and college websites have changed how we communicate with our students. Yes, students text us with questions at midnight and are indeed surprised that we haven't responded by 5 A.M. so that they can complete their paper that is due at 8 A.M. Today's communications may make students feel more connected to professors than ever before, and that means that professors are expected to spend time responding to students' questions 24/7.

How can we control the time spent communicating with students through technology and still use the mediums available successfully? Some answers might include the following:

1. Post electronic office hours. When a new semester begins, put the communications guidelines in the syllabus. For example, if you set aside 4 to 7 p.m. daily for answering e-mail, tell students that. Or, try posting when you *do not* stay plugged in to your e-mails and texts. Students should understand that not all of us stay up until 2 a.m, so tell them that no e-mails are answered between 8 p.m. and 10 a.m. the next day. Strive for some control.
2. Use your college's web-based learning management system (like WebCT or Blackboard) for as much or as little as you want, but tell students what is posted, and where, from the first day. Many professors do not give out a paper syllabus, but spend the first day of class showing students where to access it and how all aspects of the web will be used (readings, discussions, grade postings) Orientation is critical if students are to use the posted materials.
3. Remind students of FERPA (Family Education Rights and Privacy Act) regulations. Because of FERPA, college professors cannot share grades and student progress with parents, or with anyone other than the student, unless directed by the student to do so. We can't send grades via texts or e-mails, either. Grades are posted to the web-based management system. Students need reminders about proper message etiquette, so include these reminders in the syllabus and discuss them in the first class (in person or online). Discuss how students should be respectful in messages, and remind them that profanity and other negative language will not be tolerated.
4. In spite of encryption and other safety devices, electronic messages are not private. Hackers are always trying new ways to get information. Both you and students need to remember this.

5. Never write when you are angry. Imagine a student forwarding your message to your dean or provost, and you see how quickly a few angry words can get you in trouble. Actually, within an hour you could be the next big CNN story: "Professor calls struggling student a _____." Don't let it happen.
6. As professors, we work in the public eye, and our behavior will be scrutinized. Part of the scrutiny includes what we post on Facebook or any other social media. Be careful.

Administrative Support for Online and Blended Classes

Colleges and universities have jumped on the bandwagon of online courses. Some colleges have used online courses to improve revenues. Some online graduate programs actually provide additional monies and support for traditional on-campus undergraduate programs. While it is hoped that a college doesn't rush into online courses just for the revenue, many such courses cost the students as much, or more, than on-campus ones.

What kinds of questions should you ask before agreeing to teach online courses? Much technical support is needed when a course goes online, and sufficient training is needed for the instructor. Questions to ask include the following:

1. Does our campus have a computer system strong enough to support the program expected? Is the network up and running all the time, or does it experience long periods of downtime? Are the hardware and software working well and are the systems user-friendly?
2. Are the security issues of the computer system working well? Are there appropriate antivirus software and firewalls?
3. What kinds of training will I be offered before I am expected to deliver the course? How much release time will I receive to develop the course? How much course load will I be given the first time I teach the course? Many instructors say that the first time the online course is taught, they need twice the hours given for teaching the traditional course, because of all the course development and technical issues. This is in addition to release time to develop the course a semester before it is delivered.
4. Will I have teaching assistants who will help with the technology? Will they be able to help with the course content—grading assignments, answering e-mails, counseling students?
5. Will I be provided with examples of syllabi and other course materials to review before I design my course?

6. What class enrollment limits will be set? Teaching 15 students online can be very time-consuming. Imagine getting 50 in the first class. A 2009 study indicated that 77 percent of institutions surveyed reported "that they limit class size for online courses, with 37 students being the average enrollment cap" (Bart, 2009, p. 2).
7. How will I be evaluated for teaching this course? Will I see the final evaluation instrument the students complete before the class begins?
8. Once I teach this course, how many times per year will I be asked to teach it in the future?
9. May I count hours working at home as my office hours?

The Pedagogy of Online Teaching

Perhaps James Lang (2008) says it best when he writes about teaching with technology:

> And I would argue further that the basic principles of teaching and learning . . . will still operate in whatever environment we and our students find ourselves—even in the environment of online and distance teaching and learning, in which you obviously will only stand in front of your students virtually, but still need to understand the parameters of the basic teaching-learning transaction. (p. 45)

The challenge of any kind of online teaching is transferring the skills of content delivery, student engagement, motivation, and assessment into the new delivery venue.

The obstacle of time is one not to be taken lightly as you prepare to teach an online course. Brookfield (2006) writes,

> One of the greatest misconceptions about online teaching is that it is somehow a "quick and dirty" version of the much more complex reality of classroom teaching. Nothing could be further from the truth. Teachers who have taught online will usually say that their face-to-face classrooms are far less time-consuming. (p. 191)

Where should you begin when asked to deliver your course partially or completely online? Do not think that you need to reinvent the wheel. Much has been written about getting started with online teaching, and much of that has been published online. One source for information is Magna Publications, which maintains an excellent selection of materials about online teaching at www.facultyfocus.com/articles/online-education.

GETTING STARTED—PROVIDING ORIENTATION
AND EXPECTATIONS

When she was 45 years old, my sister-in-law decided to pursue her master's degree. An online program was her only option, as her job had demanding hours. She was required to take a three-hour orientation course as her first class. The course had three goals:

1. To teach the students how to be online students. This included having them practice logging in to discussion groups, making postings, submitting work, and so on. They also learned what the instructor did, what their personal advisor did, and what the tutors did. They learned who to contact with their questions.
2. To teach the students how to locate, read, and critique research in their field. My sister-in-law was quick to point out that the last time she needed to locate research, she had used a card catalog in a brick-and-mortar library, so this was all new to her.
3. To teach students how to write graduate-level papers, using the style of the American Psychological Association (APA). Citation formats have changed in the last 25 years.

The course was not easy and required her to work about 15 to 18 hours per week to complete all requirements in six weeks. However, everything she learned in the course was applicable to every other course in the program. Her future professors did not have to spend time teaching APA style or how to find a refereed article. All of that was done in the orientation class.

I share this example for two reasons. I found it fascinating that it took an entire three-semester-hour course to teach graduate students how to be students and how to get started researching and writing. If you are teaching an online course that has a prerequisite like this one, your life will be easier. If your course has no prerequisite course, be prepared to teach students the expectations of being online students and of how to research and write. I also share this example because my sister-in-law was a corporate vice president at the time she began her master's degree and was still quite unnerved by returning to school. If highly successful and competent adults are scared of taking a course, imagine the fear of a student who experienced difficulty in high school classes and is struggling for college success.

Ragan (2009) calls teaching students how to be online students "practicing proactive course management strategies." He writes that "the online classroom presents a significant shift in the understanding of roles and responsibilities on the part of both the instructor and the student" (p. 7). If you think it's hard to get students to turn in papers when you see them three times a week, imagine the challenge when you never see the students. I have talked with many professors of online courses who say that incomplete and late assignments are a major problem with this method of course delivery. Discuss deadline issues and penalties with your department and college so that online students have consistent information for each online course.

In order to help students manage time wisely and to succeed in your online or blended class, you must make the expectations crystal clear—and you must enforce them fairly. Post all deadlines from the beginning of the course. Provide criteria for papers as early as possible. Make all evaluation criteria known to students and provide students with the grading scales so that they can track their own grades. Don't change meeting times because a few students said that the posted times just aren't working. If students signed up for a class with six required online times, each one on a Wednesday from 6:30 to 8 P.M., then those expectations should be met. Changing the day or the time will not be possible.

Don't make a student's grade dependent upon other students' work or participation. This simply is not fair, yet it is done routinely in online classes. Some instructors build a participation component into the student's grade for how many times other students respond to their postings, or how many times a student responds to a posting. They defend this by saying that a strong, witty posting will garner more responses, perhaps spurring more learning. Quite honestly, students figure this out early on and make pacts to help each other out. Also, if discussions have time limits and the majority of the students in a class post late at night on the last night, a student who is not able to be up at midnight loses out. Have a grading scale where the student's work is graded on its own merit.

It is important to remember that all the regulations about teaching students with disabilities apply to online as well as on campus courses. Online students need to be provided services and accommodations that are appropriate. Students with dyslexia, reading disorders, and language disorders may need special help in their online course. Check with your college's accommodations center about help for students with disabilities who enroll in your online classes.

DELIVERY OF COURSE CONTENT

When I hear some students talk about their online courses, it sounds to me as if they received credit for just doing their homework. Indeed, some online syllabi seem to be a list of readings, followed by a list of assignments where students write chapter reviews, then complete a midterm and a final. Some courses, which cost thousands of dollars, are just making students read a textbook. Where is the teaching? Where is the delivery of content?

In my traditional campus classes, there are weekly readings, and we always use the readings in class. However, I teach so much more material than just what is presented in the readings. If I were to take one of these classes fully online, I would have to find a way to still present my material—the stories, the activities, and the supplemental content that make the course mine. I use a lot of video clips when I introduce authors and theorists. I would have to find public usage ones (such as YouTube videos), or get permission to post them for a certain amount of time on the college WebCT. (This generally means buying the site license.) I would have to record my lectures and have our information technology staff post them. It is all possible, but it takes time. I might suggest that if an instructor knows in advance that one of his or her classes is about to become an online one, that instructor should videotape every lecture during the last semester the course is taught in the classroom. This way, many of the lectures can be edited. Adding original visuals will help online students to "see" a concept.

The specifics of keeping all of the necessary content in the online course is basically a matter of course design. When designing a new course for online or blended delivery, make your goal to have a class with comparable, or better, results than the traditional one. All of the rules about course goals and student objectives hold true for online course design. Additionally, much thought has to be given to how students will participate in the class.

STUDENT COMMUNICATION

In some respects, an online course may force a student to contribute who would have just sat in the back of the class and been quiet. Some students who might have been complete wallflowers in class will shine in the online environment. The trick becomes how to help all students participate in order to learn. Of course, part of getting students to participate is how the instructors present themselves.

Conway (as interviewed in Kelly, 2009) writes that the instructor's online presence is very important to the success of the virtual class.

> Presence is more than how often instructors send out announcements, how frequently they participate in discussion forums, or how quickly they respond to student emails. Having a strong presence in an online classroom is just like a face-to-face classroom. Instructors are visible to the students and can be heard and seen. Instructors have personalities: they are open to students and are more than just a source of information. They also inspire and communicate more than course-specific content. A healthy presence in class is using the communication tools the Web has to offer. (p. 1)

Gainer (2008) finds using MySpace a "positive, appropriate tool" for building a community in a class. She sets ground rules at the beginning of each semester regarding appropriate material and "students must initiate the 'friend' request" (p. 5).

With regard to social networking, Linder (2009) reminds instructors to "be clear about your professional boundaries upfront" and "know your privacy settings" (p. 2). She further recommends that instructors ask themselves, "How much do want your students to know about you?" and "How much do you want to know about your students?" (Linder, 2009, p. 1). Before instructors go beyond the college's web-management system for communicating with students, they should also consider the fact that many students may not be using social networking sites. Yes, communication is vitally important in any college classroom, and especially so in the online environment, but the communication has to be professional in nature and in the format of delivery.

With regard to online discussions, always refer to the course goals and objectives when setting up a discussion. Requiring students to post a certain number of answers to given questions and a certain number of responses to other's postings may seem like busywork to many students. Adding requirements regarding the number of words in a response or giving points per line of a response may make the reading of discussion threads interminable. Again, students will revolt against busywork. Consider other ways to assess student achievement.

IS CHEATING EASIER ONLINE?

Cheating can be easier online, but only if the instructor allows it to be. Obviously, if students are given a test online and are not seated in a computer lab where they are monitored closely by proctors, they will use their books, notes, and friends. Instructors of online courses have to create valid assessments, knowing that these assessments are all "open book," or bring students back to campus for testing. And yes, there are some unique programs that limit how long the test is posted, how long students can work on it once they sign in, and so on, but savvy students will get a team to help them even if time and other limits are built in to the assessment. There is no way to rely on an honor code.

Few online assessments will be multiple choice or fill in the blank. More assessments will be essays, papers, and assignments constructed to very specific criteria. The old rules about changing assignments and essay questions frequently will certainly be true for online courses, as the assessments are basically public knowledge once posted. Fortunately for instructors, there are more online programs for checking plagiarism, as well.

The best advice for creating valid assessments for online courses is similar to that of creating any valid assessment. The instructor needs to make sure that the assessment is aligned to the course goals and objectives. In fact, with criteria-referenced grading, each objective has its own assessment. The criteria need to be made clear and rubrics provided for grading. When students do not know what to write about or how long an assignment should be, they will start complaining. Their complaints may start with you, but are often copied to your supervisor, their online advisor, and anyone else who may listen. Again, it is the clarity of the directions, the criteria, and the follow-through that may make or break an online course.

The Future of Online and Blended Classes

The literature about online and blended classes in higher education is nascent but growing. Imagine how much more we will know in 20 years. Right now we know that online courses are helping undergraduates and adult students complete degrees that allow them to achieve their goals. While some online programs are still looked upon with disdain by educators, more and more programs are receiving accreditation and acceptance.

My college currently offers no online courses. However, in our graduate programs, more and more classes are becoming blended, with students attending fewer classes on campus and receiving more credit for experiential learning or work done outside of class and delivered electronically to their professors. More of our undergraduates are opting to take online courses to complete some general education requirements than ever before. Online courses are popular with our students in lieu of summer courses taken at another campus.

Those who enter higher education thinking that their careers will be spent in campus classrooms in front of students may not be seeing the whole picture. The use of ever-advancing technologies will change how we teach, where we teach, and who we teach. It will be exciting to see the changes.

CHAPTER 9

Today's Students, Your Relationship with Them, and Helping Them Achieve Success

Your College Experience

Before we can understand today's college students, perhaps it is worthwhile to look at our own college experience and remember what we were going through at the time.

1. Were you an 18-year-old when you entered college?
2. Did your parents go to college? Did they pay for your education?
3. Did you work while going to college? How many hours per week? How did you spend that money?
4. Did you live on campus? Did you go back home on holidays and in the summer?
5. Did you complete college in four years? How?
6. What was your world like? What was in the news? What were students involved in? How did you communicate with friends? Did you use e-mail?

Answering "yes" to several of these questions might be indicative of a typical college experience the way it was perceived for decades. Now, think about today's students. Yes, there are still thousands of students who are traditional 18- to 22-year-old students, and whose college experience may be similar to yours. However, as more students enter college, the diversity of our students has broadened tremendously. McGlynn writes, "Today's students are different in so many ways from the students of a few decades ago" (2001, p. 36).

Who are today's students and what is their college experience going to be like? Perhaps more importantly, what are their lives like and what is their world like? How do we help them to achieve success? Is it our job to help them beyond imparting our subject matter content?

Knowing Today's Students

Every year since the late 1990s, Beloit College has released the Beloit College Mindset List. A creation of professor Tom McBride and public affairs director Ron Nief, the list informs us about what the world of 18-year-olds has been like. With reminders like, "What Berlin Wall?" and "They're always texting 1 n other," we can gain some insights into their world (www.beloit.edu/mindset/2011.php).

Much has been written about Generation X, Generation Me, and the Millennials. Writing about Generation Me, Twenge (2006) suggests that "today's young Americans are more confident, assertive, entitled—and more miserable than ever before" (cover). In a chapter titled "You Can Be Anything You Want to Be," she posits that today's students do indeed have lofty ambitions, wanting advanced degrees and professional positions (Twenge, 2006, pp. 78–79). They expect to earn a lot of money and live their dreams. Imagine the harsh reality of a student who has this mind-set, to become whatever he or she wants, and then starts college to discover that he or she can't even earn a C in a science class. Ouch! And who will these students blame for not being able to get the A in the class needed for getting into a professional graduate school? Probably the college instructor will bear the brunt of their ire, and the corresponding course evaluation will reflect it.

Howe and Strauss (2007) indicate that Generation Xers are now the parents of our students, and that "Millennial teens and collegians may be America's busiest people" (p. 42). They write that

> today's rising generation is busy—and often not in ways that today's adults can recall from their own youth. . . . Today's collegians are less likely to sunbathe idly on the campus green and more likely to hurry across it on the way to the computer lab (perhaps with an iPod in one ear and a cell phone in the other). They are less likely to play Frisbee or toss a football around, and more likely to go to the gym to run on a treadmill—or stay in the dorm and play elaborately organized videogame tournaments. (p. 44)

How does this busyness affect the students who come into our classes? They may be multitasking—reading their e-mails while sitting in class. One professor announced in a roundtable discussion, "When I asked my students to take a few minutes to read a multipage handout, one man immediately put on his earphones. I walked over and informed him that he was supposed to be reading. He then informed me that this was how he read—with music playing in his ear." Another professor added, "When I show a video clip to introduce experiments, I have one female student who instantly turns back to her computer to check her e-mail. When I approached her she said that she could certainly do both at once—and needed to in order to stay caught up. After all, she explained that she watched TV as she did all of her homework readings." Our students are busy, busy, busy—and doing two or three things at once.

While advising new students recently, I found out about an incoming freshman who was married, had young children, and decided it was time to pursue her college education. She was in her early twenties and planned to be a full-time student, while also working full-time. Her commute to campus was one hour—each way. That's a lot of multitasking for a student to do.

Many faculty report that students believe that attending class has become a personal choice for them. Students decide if what is going on in their lives is more important in the moment than that particular class. I have had students tell me that they would not be in class because their out-of-town boyfriend or girlfriend was in town that day. A student once informed me that she simply could not attend an evening class because it was Halloween, and she had to take her child trick-or-treating. Another announced to me that she wouldn't be in class because it was her first wedding anniversary. Please note that these are *not* excused absences in my class, nor are they condoned by my college. What is my response? I generally state, with a serious face, "As per the syllabus, you receive a zero for that class and you will be missing important material." I don't fight with the student or make a scene. I just state the facts. If a student asks, "Will this hurt my grade?" my response is, "Go back to the syllabus, and yes, zeros do affect your grade."

Again, there are still legions of students who are attending college and focusing on their education. Many students enter college so well-prepared with Advanced Placement classes that they can earn a bachelor's degree in three years. Others can complete college in four years and still take advantage of study abroad or internship options. Many participate in a myriad of campus activities, while some will never attend one single guest speaker or sports event. It is important for us to know our students, their backgrounds, and their worlds, but also to keep open minds about who they are. We are not to judge but to teach. It is our job to keep standards high and concentrate on the academic preparation of students. My advice to all who teach is to enjoy the diversity the students bring to class. Teach them all.

Underprepared or Unprepared Students

In an essay titled "Is College the New High School?" Richard Smelter writes, "In a few years, having a bachelor's degree will be the rough equivalent of having today's high school diploma" (2009, p. 456). He further suggests that "many more high school graduates entering community colleges won't be able to function well in advanced curriculum" (p. 456). What he doesn't say is what happens when more and more underprepared students attempt to earn college degrees at any institution.

The frustration experienced by underprepared students can manifest itself in many ways. Some of these students were successful high school students, yet are still underprepared. They have been accepted into our institutions and want all that a college diploma means. They have paid tuition and want to graduate. They want As or at least As and Bs. They may not, however, have the background and skills needed to achieve at the level to which they aspire. They may lack social skills once considered a given for college students. As college instructors, what are we to do to understand these students, support them, and at the same time maintain high academic standards? Is it our job to teach them social skills and simple good manners? These questions are not new to college instructors and are issues that are growing on many campuses.

Why do more students arrive on our campuses unprepared? There are many reasons. High schools have changed, and the rigor of the high school curriculum has changed. Reports tell us that strong students, who graduate with high grades, may only need to study two to three hours a week in high school (see, for example, Lefebvre, 2006). I have worked with college students who said that they rarely, if ever, had to study outside of school during high school.

The number of students who graduate from high school has risen. So, there are simply more students, and more of them want a college degree, along with the benefits that accompany the degree. Weimer (2002) summarizes the issue well:

> Students now arrive at college less well prepared than they once did. They often lack solid basic skills and now work many hours to pay for college and sometimes a car. Today's students are career oriented. They equate getting a good job with getting good grades. Learning is often left out of the equation. Many students lack confidence in themselves as learners and do not make responsible learning decisions. Older students return to school when their lives are already filled with jobs and families. Having little self-confidence and busy lives motivates many students to look for easy educational options, not ones that push them hard. (p. 95)

As I read this quote, I tend to agree. However, I then ask myself, "OK, they are busy with jobs and other responsibilities, but I have to teach them the skills they need for their professional career as a K–12 teacher. My colleagues are teaching the skills needed to be doctors, veterinarians, engineers, and rocket scientists. At some point can students who are so fragmented with their busy lives learn enough of the required knowledge to pursue the careers they want?"

My answer to myself is generally "no." There is a point where the fragmentation and divided attention hinders students' success, unless they do something about it. They have responsibility for their learning. We have responsibility for the classroom climate and teaching, and within that realm, what can we do to help these students?

Helping the Unprepared Students Achieve Success

As with any question about teaching in higher education, the first step is to read the knowledge base about the topic, and a knowledge base about teaching unprepared students is growing. Gabriel (2008) documents the reality of unprepared and at-risk students in her book *Teaching Unprepared Students*. She stresses that the philosophical foundations of the department, institution, and professors set the tone for student success, even the success of the unprepared student. Here are her five guiding principles for teaching all students—at risk students included:

1. All students, including those who are unprepared or at risk, can become lifelong learners.
2. Significant change requires commitment and time.
3. Struggle is a necessary and important part of life.
4. Students must accept responsibility for their learning process.
5. Professors should never do for students what students can do for themselves. (Gabriel, 2008, p. 13)

Gabriel (2008) stresses consistent contact with students, including required attendance. Of course, student attendance is enhanced when instructors know their names, help them learn each others' names, take roll, and create a respectful classroom with meaningful in-class activities (p. 41).

Knowing much about the science of teaching and learning will further help you to work with unprepared students. Gabriel (2008) informs us that

> as faculty who are experts in our fields of study and take our tacit knowledge for granted, we may fail to give students specific information on how to use learning strategies that will help them master the material in a meaningful way. While we need not be experts on the different kinds of approaches students might use for studying effectively to understand and to master course content, students nevertheless seek us out for advice on how to improve their grades. (pp. 57–58)

It is important to note that students are never, or rarely, going to tell us that they are unprepared. They will approach us in other ways, often after failing a test or receiving an unexpected low grade on an assignment. Some start the conversation by asking us for tips or hints that will help them do better the next time, when the truth of the matter is that long-term changes in how they live and study may be necessary. We may want to begin the conversation with students who are not achieving by asking how much they study and where. We may need to ask how they study, as some students do not even know how to study.

We all request that students learn the vocabulary of the subject matter we present. Science has a language all its own, for example, as do all disciplines. However, we rarely teach how to learn the vocabulary. We may actually need to teach students how to make note cards to use as flashcards to learn the vocabulary. Why didn't they learn this in their middle school or high school classroom? That's a debate for another time. At some point we have to acknowledge that they don't know this, and teach the skill as well as the content. Of course, you may work at an institution that provides a resource center that specializes in teaching students these study skills. If so, refer students, and let them know that their success in your class may depend on their constant attendance at this center.

Linehan (2007) writes, "One of the greatest gifts you can give students is to help them learn how to learn" (p. 92). While some who teach in higher education may still bristle at teaching anything other than pure subject matter content, others have learned that incorporating some learning skills may be the best way to eventually teach our content. With this in mind, let's talk about methods for guiding student production of work.

Methods for Guiding Student Production of Work

As college instructors, we want our students to complete assignments, write papers, produce projects, do lab work, practice skills, and study independently. All students, but especially the unprepared ones, may not know how to do these things. We can help them succeed with their assignments, papers, and projects by being explicit in our directions, breaking assignments down into smaller pieces that are graded, and practicing skills within the classroom. Some of the following strategies and hints are similar to ones in earlier chapters, but bear repeating for their use with underprepared students.

BEING EXPLICIT ABOUT ASSIGNMENTS

Criteria and rubrics help us to be explicit about assignments. Students shouldn't have to wonder how many pages, or how many references, or the other basics. A criteria list for an assignment prevents a student from saying, "If I had known that before I turned the paper in, I would have done it." Also, the accountability is now on the student. Some instructors may say, "But do I have to tell them everything?" Let's compare this to the real world of writing. I write for publication. When an editor accepts my idea for an article, my editor says specifically, "We need X pages, in X font, with X references, and we need it by the 30th." Giving criteria for writing actually gets students ready for the real world.

Here is an example from my discipline, teacher education:

ASSIGNMENT 1—"WHAT I TEACH AND WHY" PAPER

This paper requires you to write about the curriculum you teach as a narrative. The audience is the general public. Imagine that your paper will get read by parents of the students in your classes. The paper is worth 40 points.

1. This paper will be two to two and a half typed pages in length, 12-point font. (10 points)
2. Content (20 points). You will write about the curriculum of the class/subject you teach. You should answer the following questions:

Where does the curriculum originate? (national, state, and local examples must be included)
How much choice does the K–12 teacher have in what is taught?
How does the teacher add to the curriculum?
If a teacher wants to change the mandated, standardized curriculum, how does he or she do that?
As a teacher, how do I break the curriculum into teachable chunks/units/lessons?
Provide at least three specific examples of topics you teach at this grade level/subject area.

3. Personalize your paper (5 points). Explain what you like and don't like about the curriculum. Explain how the curriculum of your class is important for the students' lives. You may use "I" throughout the paper.
4. Grammar, spelling, and correct conventions (5 points).

Due date:

I first started this assignment years ago, and just told students to write a short paper on what they teach. I got a wide variety of papers, and they were terribly hard to grade. After giving the criteria, the papers are much better, mostly As and Bs. Am I concerned about grade inflation? No, not at all, because my students will be asked over and over in their K–12 teaching careers to do exactly what I asked them to do in the assignment—tell about what they teach and why. Teachers need to be able to do what I am having them do in class, so they better be able to do it with 80 to 90 percent mastery. What would be an example for your discipline?

Rubrics have been discussed earlier in this book. They are used more and more with college assignments. If giving an assignment for any paper or project, a rubric presents the criteria and the qualifiers for grading. A simple one follows for the previous example assignment:

Criteria	Quality Indicators
Length of paper (10 points)	10 points for 2 to 2 1/2 pages or 5 points for 1 to 1 1/4 pages or 0 points for less than one page
Content (20 points)	15 points for answering each of 5 questions (3 x 5 = 15) 5 points for adding specific examples
Personalize (5 points)	3 points for showing importance of curriculum to your students' lives and 2 points for examples from your teaching
Grammar, spelling, and conventions (5 points)	Lose 1/2 point for each grammar, spelling, or convention error

Total = 40 points

Some rubrics are much more detailed, with three to five categories across a grid indicating the quality of the indicators that make up the grade. See www.rubistar .com for more examples.

After giving the criteria or rubric, it is important to also discuss whether or not students can work together on an assignment. Remember that knowing today's students and how they work will help you to help them learn. Students will work together on assignments, and the vast majority feel that this is the best way to learn. If they don't sit down to solve problems together at a table, then they will send answers back and forth electronically. If you assign several math or science problems, students often form a little work group, divide the problems up, and then text each other the answers late into the night. If you don't want them to do this, then tell them explicitly. Remember, they will still do it—and they do not consider this cheating.

Why do students do this? It saves time, and they are busy people. So, you have to tell them that having someone else do the problem doesn't let them learn how. You have to grade quizzes and tests that are individual for a grade. On the other hand, many college instructors *want* their students to work together on the problems presented (math or otherwise). If so, tell them.

I tell students that before they turn in their papers, they should have at least two other people read their papers and help edit them. I also inform them that they may go to the college writing center and have their papers edited before they turn them in. This is not cheating—this is what professional writers do. When a student gets a lower grade because of the points lost for spelling, punctuation, or grammar issues, who is to blame? They could have had an editor in the writing center edit their paper—saving those points. I realize that if you are teaching writing conventions, you may not want to give this same advice, as you want to know what the individual knows about writing. You are the instructor—you decide, based on your goals and objectives.

Independent study, which includes problem solving and memorizing material, is important. According to Kellough and Kellough (2003), "More than ten percent of students learn best alone" (p. 248). When students learn alone, that process can take many forms—doing their homework, working online, reading, researching, or doing a hands-on, lab type of activity. The truth is that final exams are done alone, and the work that students do alone is generally what gets counted in college and in life. Students need to learn how to do things alone.

MORE GUIDELINES FOR PROJECTS AND OTHER WORK

Students learn alone and in groups. They learn by doing, so we have to give them opportunities to learn. Guidelines for projects and group work include the following:

1. The goal of the assignment or project must be clear.
2. Time frames must be stated and followed.
3. The instructor must monitor the project—including grading pieces of a big assignment or project before the final presentation (i.e., outline, references, etc.).
4. The grading and accountability must be clear. (e.g., Can we use our peers for help?)

Again, today's students are busy. They appreciate deadlines that are stated well in advance. Athletes, band members, and students who work 40 hours a week simply won't be able to complete a long project if it is given without sufficient time.

GETTING STUDENT INPUT AFTER THE FIRST PAPER, PROJECT, OR EXAM

After the first big paper, project, or exam in a class has been graded and returned, consider having students complete a short inventory or survey about their preparation and work on the paper or exam. Questions to ask include the following:

1. Were you pleased with your grade on this paper/project/exam? Why or why not?
2. How long did you study for this exam outside of class?
3. How long did you spend preparing the paper?
4. Now that we are in the third week of the semester, about how many hours a week do you spend reading the assignments and studying for this class?
5. Where and how do you study? By yourself or with others?
6. What could be done in class sessions to help you better learn/understand the material?

Getting this type of feedback may prove to be very useful to you. A colleague of mine asked similar questions after the first test and was surprised to read one student's answer: "I know I didn't do well, but I plan to buy the book soon, and that should help me with the second test."

If you ask students these questions, requesting their input, you should also be ready to implement some of their suggestions. A former student of mine told me that she could certainly do better if her current professor showed examples of the kind of lesson plans, unit plans, and curriculum maps she wanted the students to complete. In fact, the student said that she and her friends had asked the professor to do this, and the professor replied, "If you need to see examples, you shouldn't be in this course." Ouch! Obviously, the student, and her friends, went from my office to the department chair's office and then the dean's office to complain about that professor. Our students often know what would help them learn, and if they request that help, they want a response.

DON'T REINVENT THE WHEEL OR TRY TO DO EVERYTHING ALONE

You work on a campus that should be a community striving to help students succeed. Many resources already exist to help students with their learning skills.

Most campuses offer tutoring programs, help centers, and offices for those with learning disabilities. Find out about those offices and refer students to them frequently.

Attend some student events. You may discover that the star athlete who is struggling in your class must know something about the value of practice if he or she can succeed so well on a basketball court. Ask students about their study habits and work habits, and see if you can incorporate ways to study for class into their habits (online, for example).

My last comment is purely a personal one. The students sitting in your college classes will be running the nuclear power plants in the future. They will be the doctors and nurses who care for you in your old age. Their success, and their payments into Social Security from their jobs, will pay for your retirement. Now, this alone should motivate college instructors at all institutions to find better ways to help students learn.

CHAPTER 10

Instructional Management That Improves Student Behaviors

Student Incivility

Attend any conference on college teaching and you will hear stories about student incivility in sessions and in conversations in the hallways. You probably don't even have to go somewhere to hear about student incivility—just talk with your colleagues. "Courteous behavior used to be the classroom norm. It is a fact of life today, however, that common courtesy is quite uncommon" (Feldman, 2001, p. 137).

First of all, what is uncivil behavior for the college classroom? "Classroom incivility is any action that interferes with a harmonious and cooperative learning atmosphere in the classroom" (Feldman, 2001, p. 137).

In a survey, the Indiana University Center for Survey Research (2000) asked faculty to define classroom incivility by considering certain student behaviors. Some behaviors on the survey included acting bored or apathetic, making sarcastic remarks, sleeping, not paying attention, having conversations with those around them, using cell phones and computers for nonacademic purposes, arriving late, leaving early, being unprepared, taunting or belittling other students, challenging the instructor, verbally harassing other students, displaying vulgarity, and making threats of physical harm against the instructor.

It is the effects of student incivility that worry us the most. If we are intimidated, or even just interrupted, we can't teach the amount of material planned. If students in our classes are unable to learn because of other students' behaviors, then the problem is greatly magnified. Today's students want, and demand, that they get the education they are paying for, and an instructor's failure to curb disruptive students will certainly elicit complaints from the compliant, attentive students. Often, these complaints show up on end-of-course evaluations, but they may also be delivered to the department chair or dean by the student well before the course has ended.

Research by Hirschy and Braxton (2004) found that incivilities in the college classroom affect not only student achievement, but also student persistence in a class, and perhaps at an institution. They write,

> Students who frequently observe classroom incivilities may spend less energy thinking critically during the class and be less engaged with the course material afterward. It follows that being distracted from class discussions, and the concomitant connections to learning more deeply, may affect students' satisfaction of their academic and intellectual development. (p. 72)

We know from practice, and from the research, that student incivility exists. We know it can impact student engagement and achievement. Why are students exhibiting these behaviors, and how can we prevent the incivility and create the optimal learning environment?

To answer the question of why is there incivility in the classroom, we might need to ask, why is there incivility in society? It's a big question (see, for example, Bray & Del Favero, 2004, for sociological explanations of incivilities). As discussed in a previous chapter, today's students are busy, stressed, and driven to succeed, even if their previous academic preparation has been weak. Being unprepared can create additional stress that erupts in class as incivility. Some students may need attention, and negative interruptions are their way of getting it. Nordstrom, Bartels, and Bucy (2009) discuss the idea that students view themselves as consumers of education and their sense of entitlement may be an underlying cause of student incivility. It may help to review your own college experience and then consider today's students' actions as a way to build your own understanding of incivility and expectations.

Self-Inventory of College Student Behavior

1. Did you ever go to class without reading the material? Were you ever asleep or inattentive in your classes? Was anyone else unprepared or inattentive? What did the professor do about this, if anything?
2. If you received a grade of F on a quiz, assignment, paper, or exam, how did you feel? What did you do?
3. Were you ever in classes where students interrupted the instructor so much that you wanted to tell the person to be quiet? Did you feel that the person was taking away learning time from you?
4. Did you ever see a student in one of your classes be rude to a professor?

5. Did you ever want a student in the class to just leave?
6. Did you ever see an instructor completely "lose it" in front of the class? What happened? Why? What happened in the next class?

Now that you are on the other side of the desk, as the instructor, ask yourself these questions again, about your students.

1. Are your students coming to college prepared to know how to study? Do they have good study habits? What are the differences between the classroom behaviors of students with good study habits and those of others?
2. Do students come to class without reading the material? Are they ever asleep or inattentive in your classes? What do you feel you should do about it, if anything?
3. When students receive their first F, what do they do?
4. Do any students interrupt you, the instructor? Do you feel that the person is taking away learning time from the class (and teaching time from you)?
5. Do you ever want a student in your class to just leave?
6. Have you ever "lost it" in front of the class? What happened? Why? What happened in the next class?

BEING PROACTIVE VERSUS BEING REACTIVE

Considered leaders in the field of classroom management and discipline for K–12 teachers, Canter and Canter (1993) have written extensively on the need to be proactive when dealing with students of any age. If an instructor is not proactive, then he or she will certainly react when surprised by a classroom disturbance. According to Canter and Canter, reactive teachers

1. don't plan how to deal with difficult students;
2. personalize student responses (i. e., take it personally);
3. give up on students. (p. 27)

In a college classroom, a reactive teacher might become quite upset that students are having a conversation while he or she is teaching. The instructor takes this personally, gives the students the evil eye, and when their conversation does not end, stops the lecture. He or she then announces, "I was going to explain the rest of the topics in the chapter. However, since several students are talking and not listening, class is dismissed early and tomorrow there will be a quiz on the topics not covered today." The teacher's reaction is natural, feeling quite disrespected by students. He or she reacts as a human. However, this reaction punishes the other 28 students in class who were listening and trying to learn. Learning has stopped, students are frustrated, the instructor's course evaluations just went down, and the winners are the students who didn't want to be in class. In many colleges, a chair or provost would not condone this professor's behavior.

As opposed to the reactive response, a proactive instructor recognizes that student incivility may happen and plans for possible responses. Proactive teachers

1. recognize that they have a choice in how they respond to students;
2. build positive relationships with difficult students. (Canter & Canter, 1993, p. 33)

For the same example from above, a proactive teacher knows that some students will talk during lectures. The students, too, are human. (How many professors talk in faculty meetings?) A proactive teacher has stated participation expectations in the syllabus. A proactive teacher knows some initial steps to combat this talking (proximity to students, involving them in questions, simply asking them to stop talking, giving them a choice to stop talking or leave). A proactive teacher may use a wide variety of teaching strategies to actively involve students, and a proactive teacher knows when to address those students before and after class in a private conversation about their behavior.

How do we become proactive about the prevention of student incivility? Gilroy (2008) writes that as colleges grapple with incivility, "some colleges are fighting back by adopting civility statements or codes of conduct asking students and employees to accept personal responsibility for their speech and actions" (p. 37). While high schools and colleges are, and should be, different in their responses to students' misbehaviors, it may help college instructors to have an idea of what instructional management looks like in a high school classroom. High school students are used to posted rules, with positive rewards for following the rules and corrective actions, or consequences, when they don't. Let me emphasize that this is not recommended for college classes at any institution—community college or big state university. I state this because knowing what freshmen or underclass students are used to may help us understand them a little better. If a syllabus states no "rules" per se, then some students think class is a place where anything goes. After all, the rules aren't posted, and they are now paying for the experience. Students know who the teaching assistants are, who the new instructors and professors are, and some students test the limits of what they can do, with regard to in-class activity as well as grading policies.

Another example of how a recent high school graduate views the college classroom is this one. In a typical high school, if a student has an excused absence on a day when a test is given, he or she simply shows up for the next class, and asks the teacher when the test can be "made up." Generally, high school teachers must allow students to make up tests if the student was excused, and the teacher arranges time after class, or in a study hall, for the student. In essence, the burden is on the teacher. Imagine the surprise of a new college student who was out with the flu, returns to class, and asks the professor when he or she can take the exam. The professor proclaims, "There are no make-ups on exams in this course, or in college in general. Your grade was a zero on that test." How will the student react? How will the professor react when challenged?

The solution to this problem, and many others, is to state your policy in the syllabus. If there are no make-up exams, state it, and remind students of that policy before the first exam. In many institutions there are institutional policies about exams, so state the institution's policy. In some colleges, exams can be taken as "make-ups" if the student is genuinely sick, as confirmed by on-campus health services, and the instructor is informed before the test. A proactive instructor considers all of this. Of course, there are so many scenarios to consider that we can't put a policy for everything in the syllabus. As the old saying goes, "You don't know what you don't know." College departments and campuses should have discussions about incivility in all of its forms, as well as procedures for attendance and test taking.

MAKING INVISIBLE EXPECTATIONS VISIBLE

When I was an undergraduate, there was an unstated rule that if a student left an exam during the exam, he or she was finished. Fast-forward to today's students, and I can verify that they will indeed ask to leave the room during an exam to get a Kleenex or to use the restroom. During the old days, leaving the room during an exam was not allowed because it would have given the student the chance to get notes out of a pocket to restudy a few things. Today, it would open a world of online possibilities to find the answer. So, rather than assume students know that they can't leave, instructors need to post the procedures for test taking on the board or on the screen, and share them with students. Will some students think this is too juvenile, or think that they are not being treated as adults? Yes, they may. However, if one student is allowed out, others may follow, and not all to use the restroom. Students who stay in the room think that their fellow students are cheating and wonder why the instructor isn't doing anything. How you present the information makes the difference in how students feel they are treated. Presenting information in a business-like manner helps to set the tone in the classroom.

Instructional Management Strategies That Work

What high school teachers may call classroom management and discipline, college instructors refer to as instructional management. One goal of positive instructional management is to prevent, or at least curb, student incivility. There are many positive strategies, starting with things that we do before the first day of class.

While it would be nice to get our rosters and know the right students are enrolled in our classes at the right time in their academic program of studies, that is not always the case. I teach two sections of a methods course, one for elementary education majors and one for those who plan to teach in high schools. During advance enrollment, I check the roster and make sure that no elementary education majors are enrolled in the course for future high school teachers, and vice versa. If I find some students in the wrong sections, I immediately notify the students and the registrar. Of course, I keep working with the registrar and my chair to clarify the online course title and to build a system that only admits the appropriate major to the matching class, but that hasn't happened yet.

I do this exercise again one week before class starts. While it's work on my part, this makes the first day of class go more smoothly. If I started class and then discovered that six students had to be sent out of the room and go through the add/drop process to get in the other section, my first-day plans would be sidetracked. Students would be mad, and mad students cause disruptions. (I would, too, wouldn't you?) So, a first step in creating a positive classroom atmosphere is doing some administrative work well before classes start. Work closely with advisors, your department chair, dean, and/or registrar to make sure that the students are in the classes that fit their program.

THE FIRST DAY SETS THE TONE

All of the strategies listed in an earlier chapter of this book, *A Successful First Day of the Semester*, should be revisited. The first day of the semester sets the tone for the entire semester, and if the instructor doesn't set the tone, then the students will. Fred Jones, lead author of *Tools for Teaching* (Jones, Jones, Jones, & Jones, 2007), a book for high school teachers, has written about the need to not let students be the first ones in the classroom. The same can be true for college instructors, especially if we are teaching classes with predominantly new students. If the instructor arrives at the classroom before the students, he or she can set it up. The key is to get the students into the room and focused immediately on the class. Set the tone the first day by arriving early, posting a Today We Will list, and having a focus activity on the screen for all to see. This is what a proactive instructor does.

The room arrangement makes a big difference in preventing talking (and cheating). On the first day of class, make sure that all desks face forward. They do not have to be in rows, but students should not be facing each other because they will talk a lot more. If you inherit a room with tables and chairs grouped around them, restructure the room if at all possible. When you do group work, you will certainly want tables and grouping, but not at the start of the semester. Remember, you are the proactive college instructor. It is OK to ask students to help move desks and chairs, but all students should be asked to volunteer, not just males. I often get assigned a room where the arrangement is big tables with chairs around them. If I were to keep that arrangement, students' backs would be toward me. How could they possibly see me? How could I read their nonverbal expressions to check for understanding? While the tables are too big to move, I, and a couple of students, move the chairs, so that all chairs face forward. Extra chairs are stacked in the back of the room. And yes, we have to do this every class, unfortunately. I really wonder how the professor before me teaches with students' backs facing the screen. Perhaps he never uses a visual?

Routines are not ruts but provide guidelines for smooth classes. Students want structure that helps them stay focused and organized. Providing focus questions on the screen helps to start a class. Providing visuals for our lectures helps students to organize their notes. Having a set procedure for turning in and picking up papers keeps things moving along. Practice proactive steps to organizing the classroom. According to one definition, "classroom management refers to all of the things that a teacher does to organize students, space, time, and materials so that instruction in content and student learning can take place" (Wong & Wong, 1991, p. 84). While I realize that those who teach in college are hired for their expertise in subject matter, many brilliant instructors and professors may not be able to share that expertise until they master organizing the space, time, materials, and students, as this definition indicates. Many who teach in colleges and universities may fight this idea, but our prior planning and organization helps to prevent behavior issues. This, too, has become a responsibility of college instructors and professors.

USING THE SYLLABUS TO STATE EXPECTATIONS

Much has been written about the syllabus as a contract. The syllabus gives us an opportunity to state expectations, and as we introduce the syllabus, we explain our expectations. I explain the participation expectations in the syllabus by saying,

"You are adults. I know and appreciate that. Because you are adults and pay a lot of money to be here, you want to get the most out of class. When I first started teaching college students, I didn't write out expectations for participation (behavior). Then, I realized that I was keeping some hard-working students from getting the most out of classes by not stopping some interruptions and disruptions. Students complained when I didn't manage the classroom. In order for us all to be on the same page, I now make the expectations clear."

SAMPLE PARTICIPATION EXPECTATIONS FOR SYLLABI

1. Be attentive—not texting, receiving calls, checking e-mails, etc.
2. Be respectful of instructor and other students—not talking when they are or making disturbing noises.
3. Be participatory—participate in discussions respectfully, without profanity, disrespect, or incivility toward instructor or other students.

If a student is not meeting expectations, the professor may ask the student to leave that class. If asked to leave, the student may not return to class until he or she meets individually with the instructor and a dean or provost as deemed necessary by the instructor.

Why do I need the lines about what will happen if expectations are not met? Would you obey the speed limit on the highway if it were just a suggestion? Have I had to remove a student from a class? Not yet, but there was a case when I should have. So far, my intermediate steps have resolved the issue.

The intermediate steps are pretty simple, and not too confrontational. Guidelines follow:

1. Know students' names. Use proximity and privacy when talking with them about their cell phone or their talking. Don't embarrass them or they will embarrass you back, probably before the end of the class.
2. Walk over to the student. Using his or her name, state what he or she should be doing. "John, in order to learn today, you need to be listening and writing now." Pause, and when John starts to do this, say thanks and move on. Be very quiet.
3. Build a positive relationship so that you can stop talking and interrupting by saying, "Again, thanks for past comments, but I want to present new material that may answer all these questions for everyone. For special questions, see me after class." Simply quit calling on some students, and tell them as they leave the room that their in-depth questions need to be asked privately after

class and during office hours. You do have to stop some students. Be polite, but firm, and move on.

4. Start early with managing time and space. On the first day of a graduate class, I had a student pull a chair around so that she would be facing students, not me. She planned to not look at me or at the screen. I walked over, and said, "You won't be able to see my notes or video clips if you sit there. You will have to put that chair back and sit in one of the other seats." I stood. I waited. She scowled. She moved the chair. I thanked her. I didn't worry about the scowl. Fortunately, it all happened about a minute before class was to start.

5. If students start private conversations early in the semester, talk with them immediately. Don't let it slide and then expect one word to stop the problem in late October. The tone for the class is set the first day and the first week. Make it a productive one. You can always "lighten up," but it is almost impossible to "toughen up" once a few weeks have gone by.

6. Don't punish the majority who are behaving. Rather, work privately with those who are the interrupters.

7. Build positive, professional, business-like relationships with students.

8. Know college policies and know how far you can go to release students from one class session. Know who to inform if a student's behavior is so erratic that you feel he or she could become violent. Campuses have policies for student behavior in general and your knowledge of the policies will help you work with students.

9. Knowing about the behaviors caused by substance abuse may also help you to identify some inappropriate student behaviors. Don't confront the student personally, but use campus support structures to get help for the student.

Some faculty members have found that adding participation expectations in their syllabi is not enough to curb behavioral issues. They go a step further and create a contract with their students. Norin and Walton (n.d.) write, "Even in its early format, the contract positively impacted retention and behavior in the classroom as observed by us and noted by our dean. Students told us that they appreciated the precise listing of their responsibilities because it made the rules and consequences clear" (p. 12). Their contract included items regarding sleeping, inappropriate talking, rudeness, cell phone use, and disruptive behavior. Additionally, Norin and Walton included items about student responsibility for checking e-mails, getting handouts, avoiding plagiarism, and following directions. Twenty-one items appear on their published contract, which the students must sign and return to the professor.

If you decide to create a contract for students to sign, have a department chair and/or dean read it, and provide feedback, before using it. Try to limit expectations to a minimum set of statements, or rules, making the contract about behavior, not everything that could possibly go wrong in a class. When you consider the expectations you set, consider how you would feel if you were taking a class and received this list of expectations. Consider how you would feel if your son or daughter called home from college to tell you about the rules they just got in their class syllabus. In today's society, parents are hovering over their children on many campuses, and they call professors, deans, and provosts to comment on a myriad of items. Would you feel comfortable explaining your expectations to parents and a provost in the same room? If you feel comfortable explaining your expectations and consequences to all stakeholders—students, parents, administrators—then your contract is ready to use. Always remember to consider everyone who might have concerns over what you have done regarding expectations and contracts.

HOW WE TEACH IS A STRONG MANAGEMENT TOOL

Of course, how we teach remains a strong management tool. If students can't see or hear, they start doing their own thing. If they come to class and our lectures aren't related to the topics or readings assigned, they are frustrated. If the only thing that they have to do is listen, they may sleep or text surreptitiously. However, when they come to class and know that they will be actively involved, even in a large classroom or lecture hall, attention levels increase.

Much has been written about student-centered instruction, active learning, and learner-centered teaching. The earlier chapters in this book about methods for teaching address a variety of ways to teach that motivate and involve students actively. However, some faculty find that when they leave the lecture and change methods, that is when students become much more talkative and disruptive in discussions, group work, or activities.

With regard to dealing with students who over-participate, Weimer (n.d.) writes, "Address the problem using positive and constructive communication strategies" (p. 8). It is critically important to "design participation activities that require the contributions of many: small groups presenting brief reports, sharing examples, or offering summaries" (p. 8).

Again, the instructor has to manage the time, space, students, and materials of the classroom. There has to be a balance of new teacher information with application of material. No student wants to pay exorbitant tuition to attend a class where every week the students work in groups and discuss the material without any guidance or input from the instructor. Many students skip class or complain on course evaluations when too many class sessions were ones where groups presented material, and the presentations were not nearly as insightful as having the professor explain and present that material.

SUMMARY OF STEPS FOR PURPOSEFUL
INSTRUCTIONAL MANAGEMENT

1. Work with advisors and administrators to make sure the students are in the right classes before the semester begins.
2. Develop your philosophy of what a proactive college instructor/professor knows and does. Read about today's students and their needs.
3. Decide what expectations for behavior will be written into the syllabus, checking with colleagues and chairs.
4. Before the first day of class, find the room, check seating arrangements, move furniture, decide on traffic patterns to get students in and settled.
5. Arrive early to set up the classroom with a Today We Will list and a focus activity.
6. Greet students and start to build the welcoming, yet professional atmosphere on the very first day.
7. If behavior issues arise, take quick, immediate steps to stop the problems early in the semester. Use proximity and privacy to address students, and don't punish the whole class. Don't wait and hope the disruptive behaviors will go away.
8. Find teaching methods that work for your discipline and today's students. Active, participatory learning keeps students busy.
9. Use private conferences before and after class to win students over to better behavior.
10. Seek help for big issues, such as students in need of counseling.
11. Talk with your colleagues on campus and at professional meetings about the issue of incivility. Read some articles and stay current on the topic. Know today's students.
12. Consider class meetings about participation expectations. Students will tell you what they expect of their peers. Keep lines of communication open.
13. Be careful not to use sarcasm. As a rule, ask yourself, would I say this if the student's parents were in the room? If my dean were in the room? Would I want a professor to say this to my son or daughter? If the answer is "no," then don't say it.

Consider a brown bag seminar in your department where professors can share scenarios of student behaviors that are of concern. Share success stories of what works, as well. Consider some of the following for initial discussion ideas.

1. How might you handle students who never participate? Even in small classes, some students just come to class and sit. Since this isn't an overt problem, should you do anything?

2. During a discussion, a student says, "That is such a gay answer" to another student. What is the professor's response? Is this considered bullying?
3. How have you successfully handled students who monopolize time by talking incessantly to make a point before asking their question? What about a student who asks a question, then continues to talk for several minutes with his or her own hypothesis?
4. You introduce a new topic with an eight-minute video clip. As soon as the clip starts, a student starts texting. Do you respond, and if so, how?
5. How might you respond to a student who says, "I've been in bigger universities than this one, and at my last school, the professors knew this stuff so much better because they were real researchers. In fact, I studied with the co-author of our book." How is your answer different if the student says this in your office than if he or she says this in the classroom to the whole group?

Academic Integrity

When a question arises about a topic in college teaching, I refer to tried-and-true sources—McKeachie and Svinicki's (2006) *Teaching Tips* and Barbara Gross Davis' (2009) *Tools for Teaching*. However, with regard to academic integrity, I was surprised to find quotes from Fredericks' (2007) *The Complete Idiot's Guide to Teaching College* to introduce this section. Fredericks writes that many new professors might be quite surprised at the level of cheating that takes place in higher education.

- Numerous studies have found that from 40 to 90 percent of all students cheat on classroom tests.
- Several studies have shown that between 75 and 98 percent of college students surveyed each year report having cheated in high school.
- In one national survey of over 2,000 undergraduates, more than 50 percent admitted to cheating, and half of those admitted to cheating more than once. (p. 226)

We tend to know why students cheat—peer pressure, pressure to achieve, low self-esteem, feeling that they won't get caught, and it's easy (Fredericks, 2007). We also know how they cheat—downloading Internet articles and pasting whole sections into papers, looking at another's paper in an exam, copying facts and formulas on to clothing or bottles before an exam, and simply paying others to write their papers (Fredericks, 2007). The trickier question is how to prevent cheating. Again, to quote Fredericks (2007), "The prevalence of cheating on college campuses makes it seem like a virulent disease—one impossible to totally eradicate. Yet, we can implement practices and measures in our courses that will significantly reduce the 'need' to cheat by students and establish an atmosphere that values honesty and academic integrity" (p. 228).

McKeachie and Svinicki (2006) write that an instructor can lower pressure in a course by having "a number of opportunities for students to demonstrate achievement of course goals, rather than relying on a single exam" (p. 116). Obviously, having several chapter exams over smaller amounts of material can be less stressful than just one midterm and one final over huge amounts of material. These authors stress that assignments that are too long or tests that cover too much trivial knowledge will cause the frustrated and desperate student to resort to cheating. Lastly, McKeachie and Svinicki (2006) relate that "cheating will occur if the instructor seems unconcerned" (p. 117). So—proctor those exams with active walking around the room and monitoring. It's old-fashioned, but it works.

Davis (2009) writes, "General admonitions to 'avoid cheating' are relatively ineffective" (p. 345). However, it does help to teach students what is "acceptable and unacceptable behavior by giving examples of plagiarism, impermissible collaboration, and other practices" (p. 345).

Guidelines and points to consider for encouraging academic integrity follow:

1. Know your campus' guidelines and procedures on academic integrity. This may include an honor code policy. Whatever the policies are, include them in your syllabi and discuss them with students early in the semester.
2. Even more important than early discussion of policies is a reminder before the first big paper or before the midterm. Remind students of your policies, such as not leaving the room during an exam and when working together is accepted and when it's not.
3. On exam days, arrange the room in rows, with all students facing front, and write the procedures for test taking on the board. These may include the reminders that all books and backpacks must be closed and on the floor. No electronic devices may be used or turned on during the exam. No hats. No sunglasses. No drinks (as bottles may have the answers written on the labels).
4. Proctor exams. Tell students that you are proctoring. Walk around the room; don't sit at a desk in the front of the room. If you sit, sit at the back so students can't see where you are looking. Be proactive about where you are and what you are doing. Tell students ahead of time that you don't help them during exams, or they will ask.
5. When papers are due, allow a lot of time for students to write them. Give all of the criteria for a major paper weeks before it is due. I write professionally, and I can only write about 10 pages in a day after all the research is done.

Your students rarely have a whole day to devote to writing for your class, so allow them time.

6. If you are grading group work, know that students worked together, and an individual's score may not be a valid indicator of his/her own learning. It is better to use groups for informal purposes and to grade the work of individuals that may come from brainstorming or group discussions.

7. No matter what you say, homework will be done with others, and students will use the Internet and former students for answers. Know that this happens. Once the homework is handed in for a grade, you just have to accept that the student whose name is on the paper gets the credit. Of course, when you put the same problems on in-class quizzes and tests, you will see who learned the material for themselves.

8. The best prevention for plagiarism and copying is to create criteria and rubrics that do not lend themselves to run-of-the-mill papers. Create the questions that you want answered in the paper. Require specific references from the readings in your class for a certain number of points. Requiring specific references and putting conditions on the age of references makes it harder for a student to purchase an online paper.

9. When you are in doubt about what a student has written, go online and check on one of the websites designed for catching plagiarism. Some campuses use text-matching software for this purpose and all professors can access the software. Ask a student about how they researched their paper before going to the authorities. I once did this and a student replied that since she wasn't a teacher, she called a friend in California who was and got most of the ideas for the paper from that phone call. I said that was a good idea, but that she needed to document the call and the friend, or it was plagiarism. She added a new intro, another reference, some additional discussion, and it became a good paper. She said she didn't know that a conversation had to be cited as such. She learned, and that's what we want.

10. While it will mean more work for you, rewrite tests and change written assignments from semester to semester. Create a pool of assignments, and one of test questions, and then make assignments and tests from those pools. When you return graded exams to students, do not let them keep the tests. Files of old tests, by course and instructor, are kept in study rooms of dorms, sororities, and fraternities.

11. Be aware when a paper just doesn't "sound" like the rest of the student's work. If the paper is much better, or even much worse, it may not be original work. Knowing the students and establishing relationships early will help with combating cheating and plagiarism.

12. When cheating or plagiarism occurs, get back-up help. Do not confront students in front of peers. Collect papers, make notes, and deal with the

problem immediately, but privately, and with the support of your chair, dean, and other institutional personnel. Always make copies of papers and tests. Keep notes of occurrences.

13. You must follow your institution's policies. Keep all administrators informed throughout the process.

14. If it is not clear that a student has cheated or plagiarized but you think he or she may have, consult a colleague or administrator before going to the student. Davis (2009) writes, "Avoid using incendiary words. Instead of *cheating* or *plagiarism*, discuss *copying* or *insufficient citation of sources*" (p. 358).

15. It can be really helpful to have a colleague sit in on a student conference with you. In some institutions, this colleague may be a dean of students or other support person who specializes in student affairs. Do not hesitate to get back-up help when needed.

Most importantly, keep discussing academic integrity as a faculty, both within your department and campus wide.

CHAPTER 11

Earning Promotion and Tenure

> The faculty in American colleges and universities have always been the heart of the institutions where they work, the intellectual capital that ensures those institutions' excellence. The quality of the faculty relates directly to the effectiveness of a college or a university in facilitating students' learning, creating new knowledge, and linking research and practice in ways that benefit society. (Gappa, Austin, & Trice, 2007, p. xi)

While you are understandably concerned about being rehired and eventually earning tenure in your institution, imagine for a moment the institution's concern about having enough qualified faculty members to staff every class. The institution invests a lot of time and money in hiring new faculty, and from an administrator's perspective, the best possible outcome for a new hire is success. When a new hire leaves, or is asked to leave, the laborious search process must begin anew, costing thousands of dollars and hundreds of labor hours for faculty and administrators. Recognizing that your employer wants you to succeed may help you battle those "what happens if" fears.

What Is Tenure and What Does It Mean?

It is important to note that tenure is mutually beneficial for the faculty member and for the institution. Tenure gives the faculty member job security and the institution a sense of employee stability. As defined by the American Association of University Professors in 1940, tenure served as the way to ensure academic freedom "through an employment contract that guaranteed permanent or continuous employment and due process in the event of termination for cause"

(Gappa et al., 2007, p. 128). Yes, tenured professors can still be released, but the institution must follow due process and have a cause for release. Before tenure is granted, institutions may release instructors and professors without stating cause—a contract is simply not renewed.

An important side note to make at this time is that a great number of people teach in higher education and are not in tenure-track positions. Some institutions simply do not have a traditional tenure system, while others are hiring more and more visiting professors, adjuncts, and instructors. Why? Financial issues are one concern, as tenure-track employees command the best salaries. An inability to control enrollments or ups and downs in enrollments may enter into hiring decisions. Read the *Chronicle of Higher Education* (see www.chronicle.com) for recent articles about life on the tenure track and the workplace of the non-tenure-track employees.

Whether you are tenure track or not, you will be evaluated for reemployment wherever you work, and this chapter outlines strategies for keeping your job and earning tenure when available.

The Big Three—Teaching, Scholarship, and Service

Teaching, scholarship, and service are the areas in which college professors are evaluated. It is patently obvious that we are supposed to teach well to be instructors and professors at all levels of higher education, but what defines *well enough*? Scholarship is the broad term for research and publications, and the quality and quantity of scholarship required is determined by the type of institution and its culture. Service is interpreted differently at each institution. At some colleges, service implies service to the college itself, and that service is fulfilled by sitting on committees and volunteering at college functions. At other institutions, a professor may only meet the service criteria by serving the profession, as evidenced by work at the state and national levels, in addition to service to the college.

No matter your job title—instructor, adjunct, visiting, or assistant professor—the first step to positive evaluations and continued employment is simply finding out what you need to know. The evaluation criteria may be published online, and you should read it before you attend the interview. You will be a well-prepared candidate if you say, "I've read the tenure and promotion criteria online, and I have a couple of questions about it." If the information was not available before the interview, then ask diplomatically at an appropriate time during the interview.

Your job interview should include a session with a chair, dean, or provost whose job it is to explain the evaluation criteria to you. Ask the faculty you meet about criteria for promotion and tenure, as you want to hear both the formal explanation and what those in the trenches have to say. The criteria should be published and you should have a copy before you ever sign a contract.

Once hired, you should be given orientation about how you will be observed and evaluated. This should be a fairly formal process, done during new faculty meetings, or provided by the college's center for teaching support. If you don't receive this information, ask for it. You are already seeing a trend here—you have to ask to find out what really happens. As a new faculty member, you may be assigned a mentor, and that person can be a good source of all of this information.

Most colleges offer seminars and workshops on how to prepare your materials for evaluation. These sessions may be as simple as a brown bag discussion where new employees bring a sack lunch and hear a panel of their peers discuss how they passed their third-year review or how they prepared their tenure and promotion materials. Attend these sessions and keep asking questions. When it actually comes time to prepare a dossier or portfolio for your review, look at samples from previous professors who were successful.

If the first big piece of advice is to ask, ask, ask, then the second piece of advice is to read. As academics, we should recognize that there is a knowledge base for just about everything, including how to get tenure. Read the *Chronicle of Higher Education* (www.chronicle.com) as well as other sources. Consider James Lang's (2005) book *Life on the Tenure Track: Lessons from the First Year*.

EVALUATION OF TEACHING

Yes, successful college instructors must teach well. What is good teaching and how is one's teaching evaluated for its acceptability? Ask 10 educators to define good teaching and you will get 10 very different answers. Good teaching means good lectures, some will say. Others will say that good teaching is evidenced by active learning activities in the classroom. Do good grades earned by students indicate good teaching? Or, does giving a range of As to Fs indicate that you were a tough (good) teacher? How much input do, and should, students have in deciding if you are a good teacher? Three common ways of evaluating teaching effectiveness include observations by others, student course evaluations, and performance assessment documented in a dossier or portfolio.

OBSERVATIONS OF YOUR TEACHING

Being observed probably scares even the most experienced teachers. However, turn the observation around and ask yourself, "Would I want my child in a college classroom where no one ever observed or monitored the professor's teaching?" There are various models for the supervision of instruction in a classroom. One is facetiously called the "gotcha" observation. In a gotcha observation, the supervisor makes unannounced visits, usually with clipboard in hand, and sits in the back of the room, looking for things to write down that indicate they "got you" doing something you shouldn't have been doing. Hopefully, your evaluators have better sense than to approach your observations in this manner.

Many observations fit what is called clinical or collegial supervision (see, for example, Glickman, Gordon, & Ross-Gordon, 2008). With this model, a supervisor holds a pre-conference to ask about your teaching and to plan for an observation. The observer generally asks about the class, what topics you are currently teaching, and when an observation can take place. The observer/supervisor should ask what your specific goals and objectives are for the class, and what you want them to watch for with regard to instruction or student behavior.

For example, if you teach a large section of underclass students and have been concerned about student participation, you might tell your observer that you have been working on asking more open-ended questions to elicit responses and that he or she should observe and record how you ask the questions throughout the class. After the observation, you and the observer sit down and have a post-conference, where the observer shares objective data—like number of questions asked in 50 minutes and number answered by students—and then you both discuss what you, the instructor, will do next. The purpose of clinical supervision is to support you and to help you to improve, yet the observer is still evaluating your teaching.

Another staple of observations is the checklist. The supervisor has a checklist of required components that he or she needs to see in order for you to have a positive evaluation. What might be on a checklist?

1. The instructor arrived on time and began class punctually.
2. The instructor was organized and prepared for the class.
3. If visuals were used, they supported the lecture and were clear for all to see.
4. Instructor comments to students were appropriate (not negative or sarcastic).
5. When possible with class size, the instructor knew and used student names.
6. The curriculum of the class was appropriate.
7. The instructor's voice was clear and easy to understand.
8. Students' questions were encouraged and were responded to by the instructor.

If a shortened checklist with room for qualitative comments is used, it might look like this:

A. Evidence of instructional time used purposefully.
B. Evidence of a positive classroom climate established.
C. Engaging lecture and/or activities provided that meet the curriculum appropriately.
D. Evidence of ongoing/formative assessment of student learning.

Then, after writing examples for each point, the observer might write strengths and suggestions for improvement.

Marzano (2009) has published "a comprehensive list of strategies that relate to effective teaching" (p. 33). Your institution may use a published checklist or guideline for evaluating instructors. Some of the strategies on Marzano's list include the following:

1. Teacher identifies critical information.
2. Teacher organizes students to interact with new knowledge.
3. Teacher asks questions that require students to make and defend inferences.
4. Teacher engages students in cognitively complex tasks.
5. Teacher provides clear learning goals.
6. Teacher understands students' interests and backgrounds.
7. Teacher scans the room to monitor students' level of engagement.
8. Teacher maintains a lively pace. (p. 33)

If your institution has a form for observations, you should definitely see it before you are observed for an evaluation. Perhaps a mentor can observe with the same instrument as a practice for your first formal observation.

Another form of observation is the three- to five-minute walk-through. With this system, the same administrator walks into your class from time to time and only stays a few minutes. The administrator records what you are doing (lecturing, asking questions, working with small groups) and observes what the students are doing (paying attention, sleeping, volunteering to answer questions). Because the observations are short, the observer may just catch you at a bad time. However, if the observer is using this style of observation, he or she should see some patterns over time.

Self-governance plays a huge role in higher education, so many times your observations will be completed by other teaching colleagues, whose evaluations in the tenure process are considered. Being observed by colleagues has advantages and disadvantages. A colleague in your field is the better evaluator of the curriculum being taught. Imagine a new professor of German being observed by those who did not speak German. Would they know if he or she were teaching the grammar correctly? The disadvantage of being observed by colleagues is that they may have little or no training in how to observe someone for an evaluation.

Their teaching styles may be drastically different from yours, and they may give you a weak evaluation because you do not teach as they do.

I was once observed by a colleague who was appalled that I did not take roll by calling names aloud and make dramatic gestures when a student was not there or comment to a student who was absent during the previous class. I started my class by having students write a warm-up activity, and then I covertly took attendance while they worked. By two minutes after the hour, we could start a meaningful discussion of the focus question that was the warm-up activity. My method for taking roll was research based. I still wonder what his reasoning was for belittling students in public for their past absences and using five minutes to make a production of roll. Worse yet, why did my chair think his style of running a class was one that should be used by me?

Observations of teaching are one way to evaluate teaching effectiveness, even if the definition of effectiveness varies and instructors' styles vary widely. Find out how you will be observed, by whom, how often, and when. Have a lesson plan ready to give to the observer so that he or she may follow your class more easily. Ask to discuss the observations, and ask for copies of the observer's form and/or comments. Keep this documentation.

STUDENT COURSE EVALUATIONS

Your teaching will be evaluated by your students. In some institutions, we earn tenure or are denied tenure in a large part due to these evaluations. Again, every institution varies in how it uses student evaluations. A typical student evaluation might ask students to rate the following aspects of the course on a scale of 1 to 5:

1. The teaching materials were helpful (textbook, handouts, online).
2. The course objectives were clear and were followed by the instructor.
3. The exams, papers, and projects reflected the course content.
4. Exams and papers were graded and returned in a timely manner.
5. The instructor communicated the subject matter well.
6. The instructor was prepared for each class.
7. The instructor's use of learning technologies (online, videos, etc.) enhanced the class.
8. The instructor was respectful of students' questions.
9. The instructor encouraged students.
10. The instructor was available for help outside of class.
11. Overall quality of this course.
12. Overall quality of the instruction.

Qualitative comments are often solicited on the student course evaluation. Students may be asked to list strengths and weaknesses of the course and of the instructor. They may be asked to describe their recommendations for the course.

When students are asked to evaluate their courses and their instructors, many take the evaluation seriously and write constructive criticism and valid feedback. However, a student who took a course out of sequence or who was totally unprepared for a course may use the course evaluation to vent his or her frustrations. While it has probably been researched, we can guess that students anticipating an A will generally be more positive about a course than a student who fears a low grade.

What can we do to improve student course evaluations? Make sure that students are in the right classes at the right times. Provide feedback to students about their grades early in the semester, so that students who really shouldn't be there can drop the course. Some institutions allow the instructor to hand out his or her own evaluations and then just step out into the hallway while students complete them. It might be better to ask a colleague to give your evaluations, while you proctor his or hers, to prevent a student from leading peers to negative comments.

Students are very stressed at final exams, so give the evaluations on the last day of class. Allow students time to write their evaluations. If you don't like the institution's student evaluation form, join the committee that reviews it. If you want to create an additional one that better evaluates the types of things you stress in the course, you may, but you will still have to give the mandated one and follow your institution's procedures. Some instructors provide pizza or snacks the last day, but honestly, I don't know of any research that proves this helps. Your thorough organization and preparation for each class will help you to get strong evaluations.

When you get the results of course evaluations back, read them and try to keep an open mind. If you feel a need to write a response about student comments, there should be a way to do that. I once had a student write that I did not meet her expectations because I did not cover how to be a curriculum director in my graduate curriculum class. I was dumbfounded, as two whole classes were devoted to that exact topic. Additionally, I gave many assignments that were the types of things curriculum directors do, such as writing curriculum maps. I finally decided that the comment had to have been written by a student who had very poor attendance, and who was mentally not in the class when she was physically present. However, the comment did lead me to be even more explicit in explaining why we did each assignment. There will always be outliers from student evaluations, but hopefully valid patterns will emerge that help you to improve your teaching and meet student needs.

PORTFOLIO AND DOSSIER DOCUMENTATION OF TEACHING

When a colleague or supervisor observes my teaching, he or she might not be able to see some of the items on which I am being evaluated. A better way to demonstrate some of the items might be through portfolio documentation. To determine if an instructor writes a clear syllabus, a syllabus should be available for review. The same is true for tests. To evaluate if a group project meets course objectives, the explanation of the project, along with the criteria sheet and grading rubric, can be placed in a portfolio. Promotion and tenure dossiers may require a sample of syllabi and exams. Adding some student work may also be appropriate (with the permission of the student and with name removed for confidentiality reasons). Keep good files with any paperwork that may be required of you later.

SCHOLARSHIP—RESEARCH AND PUBLISHING

If your institution evaluates only your teaching and service, then you get to skip this section of the chapter. However, most four-year institutions require scholarship in the form of publications, and often in a substantial amount. It is critical to know and thoroughly understand the publishing requirements before taking a position. Some institutions may spell out requirements—for example, three nationally peer-reviewed articles a year and a book before earning tenure, or one article a year and evidence of national conference presentations. Sometimes a minimum number of publications required for tenure is not written down, but a college faculty handbook may state that the employee must have an ongoing research and publishing agenda. Some institutions only count "top-shelf" publications and might give no credit for an article published in a state or regional journal. Online publishing has been around for quite a while now, and some disciplines may have predominantly online journals. The rules and expectations vary widely, not only from institution to institution, but also from department to department within the institution.

How does one get started in publishing? The research from the dissertation (master's or doctoral level) is a starting place for most people. Take the basic findings from your research and write it up in the style of an article and start submitting it. Actually, many new professors begin their first tenure-track job with publications that they have made with one of their primary advisors. The new professor may co-write with the advisor or the advisor may help to get an article published by providing contacts with editors. Your doctoral advisor can make a huge difference in whether or not your publishing career is jump-started.

Getting published is all about writing for the audience. Know the requirements for a journal before you start the article. Read widely in your field and know the tone of the articles in each journal. Go online and read each journal's guidelines for authors. Talk with colleagues about where they have published. Networking is critically important. In my field, education, there are generally sessions on writing for publication at all of our national conferences. Attend those sessions and do exactly as the editors instruct. Start reviewing for journals, if invited. Just getting to know the editors may help, as they may recognize your name when your piece is submitted, but don't be a pest.

Never submit a piece that hasn't been read and edited by several people. A friend of mine says that she self-edits by reading her articles aloud. It helps her to find funny typos like "the students is." Some institutions provide editing for you, through a teaching support center or the library. After you have submitted an article, keep good records of when the article was submitted, and check back after time has passed. While some journals take years from the time you submit until you see your article in print, you do need to follow up with journals to make sure your piece hasn't been lost. Follow the directions of the editors and do as their guidelines and letters state. If an article is accepted conditionally or you are asked to resubmit for consideration, do it. There is no way to get published if you don't resubmit. Get over the hurt and the pride issues and do what the editors want. When you are mega-famous, you can do it your way.

FINDING THE TIME TO WRITE

How does one find the time to write? The answer is, how badly do you want to keep your job? I went to a conference where a speaker said, "We all have 24 hours in a day and seven days in a week. You decide which times you will write, but decide." Everyone's research and writing schedule is different. Some professors receive release time specifically for research and writing, and their course load is lightened by one class a semester. During that semester, they budget more time to write. I have long designated Wednesday as my writing day. My classes are on the other days of the week. In my college, there are often Friday afternoon meetings, so Wednesday just works best. I don't grade papers on that day or read e-mails, either, until I have met my writing quota. I know professors who get up early to write, or who stay up late to write several days a week, but I just can't do that. I find blocking my time works much better. I also write and/or grade papers and prepare lessons on Sunday afternoons. As the president of my college once said, "The nice thing about college teaching is you can decide which 50 or 60 hours a week you want to work."

Some professors find publishing easier if they collaborate with colleagues. Others find this doesn't work at all. You have to know your colleagues before you decide to take on a research and writing project with them. When your tenure and promotion materials are considered, committees may evaluate your publications with different weights depending on single or joint authorship. Obviously, coauthoring a piece with a big name in your field will work in your favor. Being the last name on the list of authors on every publication on your résumé may significantly hurt you. If your discipline lists multiple authors of a single article by alphabetical order, you would need to explain that in documentation for a campus-wide promotion committee, as it is generally accepted that the first author listed is the lead author.

GRANT WRITING AS SCHOLARSHIP

In the sciences and engineering, grant writing has long been a necessary component of research and publication, as success in obtaining funds to support research is critical. Grant proposal writing, and the winning of grant funds, has become a component of most other disciplines, as well.

Just as with general research and writing for the demands of journals, those who win grants have found out about the specifics of the grant programs and have tailored their proposals to meet the requirements. Teams of researchers often band together to write successful grant proposals.

A university may give credit toward promotion and tenure just for writing a proposal and submitting it. More credit is given to proposals that are accepted. Those who win large grants often have buy-outs of their contracts and spend less time teaching and more time in grant-funded research. Publishing should be a given once the research of a grant-funded proposal is completed. In fact, writing the final report to the grant funder may be considered a publication.

Some other types of reports may also be considered publications by the institution. Some professors in professional schools of education are given release time to write their state or national accreditation reports. These lengthy documents should definitely be listed on your vita and be substantiated in the final documentation for promotion and tenure.

SERVICE

The third leg of the evaluation process is that of service. A cynical professor might say that teaching at the institution should be service enough, but just as the publication requirements seem to be ever increasing, so, too, are the demands placed upon professors to serve.

I estimate that I spend a minimum of two to eight hours a week in meetings. I serve on both school and college-wide committees. My campus service has included the following committees in the last 12 years: faculty development, Center for Teaching Excellence advisory, international programs, budget, promotion and tenure, graduate school, planning council, academic council, undergraduate research, hearing/grievance, and a large number of faculty and administrative job searches. I have chaired several campus-wide committees, and I served as the chair of faculty assembly one year. Of course, there are monthly departmental, school, and graduate faculty meetings. Since I teach at a small college, faculty are expected to work at least one Saturday a semester at a college recruitment day, and each faculty member must attend graduation each semester, also on a Saturday. Volunteers are sought for sponsoring student clubs and for assisting in some college events, like serving pancakes to students during finals week and greeting alumni at homecoming. This type of service is reported in annual evaluations, as well as in promotion and tenure dossiers.

At some institutions, the service to the institution is just a start, and the real "points" for promotion and tenure come from service to the community or to one's state and national professional association. Serving on editorial boards, boards of directors, and national committees is the way to earn tenure at some colleges and universities. In most professional associations, one can be appointed to committees but must be elected to national offices. It can be difficult to be appointed or elected, and the work is quite time-consuming.

I have reviewed dossiers of professors applying for promotion and tenure who also report volunteer work in the community—everything from speaking at a Rotary Club meeting to working in a soup kitchen. Many in higher education sit on community boards, such as the Red Cross. Some institutions count this type of volunteer work highly when reviewing a dossier for promotion and tenure. Other institutions do not and want to see lengthy publication lists.

With all of the requirements for teaching, research, and service, a new faculty member must prioritize. In a book chapter titled "Knowing About and Getting Tenure," Vick and Furlong (2008) write, "Concentrate on research, publication, and teaching—in that order" (p. 225). However, they also point out that "the tenure process is different in each institution, and it is important that you learn what the process is for you" (p. 226). The key is to know what your institution requires and then prioritize to get it done in a timely manner.

THE UNSPOKEN FOURTH CRITERIA—INSTITUTIONAL FIT

While not on a university's evaluation form, institutional fit is often considered by some administrators as they evaluate all instructors for rehire. One often hears of an outstanding professor, with an earned doctorate, who is fantastic at being in front of the class and teaching, but who just does not publish. This person needs to be teaching at a college where there is no writing requirement and where his or her teaching is needed and rewarded. The opposite is also true. There are some brilliant researchers who excel in their labs, but who have difficulty delivering content to undergraduates. These people need to find research positions where teaching means leading small seminars to those interested in learning about their research.

While many reading this will agree with what I have said, others will say, "Well, the institution says one thing and does another." It is tough to be at an institution that says it values teaching first and foremost, only to learn that writing four articles in six years is not enough for earning tenure. The best advice about institutional fit is to have the difficult conversations about all of the criteria for retention in the job early in your career. The more you know about the expectations, the better prepared you are to meet them.

HOW TO DOCUMENT AND SHOWCASE YOUR WORK

There is an old Mac Davis song that begins with the lyrics, "Oh Lord, it's hard to be humble, when you are perfect in every way." Whether you are undergoing a half-hour interview with your boss to review your work for a one-year contract or coming up for promotion and tenure, it's not about being humble or about being egotistical. It's about documenting your work so that all who evaluate you know you have met the required criteria.

There are two things to remember—your work must meet the standards, and the documentation must also. Some people teach, publish, and serve, but are not good record keepers. This alone may keep them from earning what they seek. On the other hand, a beautiful dossier that does not include minimum requirements for publishing, but tries to steer the reader to overlook that fact with a preponderance of service projects, will not win you tenure, either.

Whether your institution calls this collection of documents a portfolio or a dossier, make sure you know the requirements years before the final one is due. By collecting the necessary pieces of your dossier as each year goes by, and by keeping the pieces in an organized manner, the organization of the final product will be much easier. In general, you need to keep all of the following:

1. Copies of all student course evaluations, both quantitative and qualitative.
2. Copies of all class observations completed by chairs, deans, and colleagues for your evaluation.
3. Sample copies of syllabi and exams.
4. A running list of which class sections were taught each semester and how many students were enrolled. Include summer classes.

5. Letters of acceptance of articles from professional journals.
6. A copy of the title page and abstract of all publications.
7. Sample copies of key articles.
8. Pages from professional conference programs where you have spoken.
9. Evaluations of professional conference presentations from attendees, if available. (Some disciplines do this.)
10. Documentation of campus committee work (often a thank-you letter or e-mail from the committee chair).
11. Documentation of state and national professional organization work (again, a thank-you letter or e-mail is often fine).
12. Letters indicating grants won and other awards received.

A good dossier is not just a scrapbook. You should include narrative cover pages as requested by your institution that explain the artifacts you are using for documentation. In my college, a two- to three-page narrative explains each of the three categories—teaching, scholarship, and service—and introduces the documentation. Since professors from many disciplines will read a dossier, it is important to use these cover sheets to explain what is common or uncommon about certain publications. For example, in teacher education, one of our top-tier journals is not refereed. However, when I created my promotion dossier, I included a list of all the journals in my field that showed the acceptance rates of the nonrefereed journals. When a colleague sees that a journal in which you are published is international in scope and has only a 5 percent acceptance rate, that is powerful.

Each college and university will have its own set of requirements for documentation. Some specify the type of binder that must be used and further specify that all documentation must fit in that binder. Some have required forms for documenting years of service and committee work. Members of the promotion and tenure committees are generally expected to reject any dossiers that don't fit the standards. In order to get the promotion, tenure, or job renewal you seek, follow the rules.

CHAPTER 12

Career Stages

People's career paths fascinate me. I am always interested in stories about how a stockbroker becomes a llama farmer, a department store buying executive becomes a third-grade teacher, or a school's custodian becomes its principal. Stories of how people become teachers in higher education are equally fascinating. In my field, teacher education, most of us teach in elementary, middle, or high schools for several years; earn our advanced degrees; and then start teaching people to do what we used to do. Other disciplines are similar—doctors teaching people to be doctors, lawyers teaching people to be lawyers.

Professors of business have often been successful business owners or managers prior to teaching, psychology professors may have started their careers with private practice, and many English professors are legitimate authors. Some college professors have gone through college for years as graduate students and then decide that college is where they want to stay—teaching and researching. The real world eludes them. This can be both good and bad. It's good when someone with extensive learning can communicate that discipline's knowledge base to others and can create new knowledge in the field. Many great professors spend their whole lives in the ivory towers of higher education and the world is a better place because of their deep study and contributions to true knowledge. It's bad if the person just lives in the world of books and can't relate the knowledge base to today's students. Think about your former college professors. How did they get to be where they are and how might their path have influenced yours?

The world of higher education really does change, as does society. Author Daniel Pink has written the following:

> The last few decades have belonged to a certain kind of person with a certain kind of mind—computer programmers who could crank code, lawyers who could craft contracts, MBAs who could crunch

numbers. But the keys to the kingdom are changing hands. The future belongs to a very different kind of person with a very different kind of mind—creators and empathizers, pattern organizers, and meaning makers. These people—artists, inventors, designers, storytellers, caregivers, consolers, big picture thinkers—will now reap society's richest rewards and share its greatest joys. (2005, p. 1)

In the vein of Pink's paragraph, I think that the future of higher education will depend not only on the bright minds who are attracted to teaching there, but on those individuals' abilities to actually teach. We may see more caregivers and consolers in higher education, as the job of teaching in colleges and universities will require being able to meet all the needs of students, not just passing along information. With this potentially new paradigm to consider, what might your career path look like in higher education, and what can you do to stay current and progress through your career productively and happily?

Much has been written about the career stages of K–12 teachers. Steffy (1989) characterizes a teacher's career stages as anticipatory, expert/master, renewal, withdrawal, and exit. In a later work, Steffy, Wolfe, Pasch, and Enz (2000) name the stages novice, apprentice, professional, expert, distinguished, and emeritus. If one is hired as a professor in a tenure-track position, there are already set stages—assistant, associate, and full professor. At each stage, certain expectations must be met for promotion. Rank and privileges are bestowed. Raises are given.

I like to think of a career path in higher education in a light other than just rank, privileges, and raises. This chapter will discuss career stages I have named new and enthusiastic, experienced, deep contributions, and elder statesperson. For each stage, I will present advice one might hear, comments on what one should be doing, and what professional development opportunities can help the instructor improve and grow at that stage. Moving into administration will be discussed in some of the stages and as a stage of its own.

New and Enthusiastic

At a recent conference, I met a woman who had been plucked from the world of business to teach at a community college. Lovely and outgoing, she was at the conference to "learn how to teach in higher education." She had completed one semester of teaching in her field, and said, "I discovered I love this, but I don't think I really know how to do it. I am simultaneously trying to figure out how to teach while teaching full time." Before simply advising her, I asked her plans for her own professional development. "I've picked my doctoral program, and I know I will keep attending conferences like this one about college teaching."

A pretty good plan, all things considered. She will be very busy over the next few years, teaching full time and earning her doctorate. I also advised her to read widely about college teaching and to consider taking a methods course. If her institution didn't offer one in methods of college teaching, she might even consider auditing an education class on methods of secondary teaching.

We all know bright-eyed, young PhDs who want to do everything—teach well, write prolifically, and join every committee. We should encourage their unbridled enthusiasm and support their efforts. In my first job after completing my doctorate, my dean said, "I so enjoy working with new hires who haven't had the enthusiasm and optimism beaten out of them yet by the institution." What an interesting—and depressing—line! Institutions should be places that respect their employees and provide a supportive, nurturing environment for all.

What resources should be available to support new faculty? As the director of my college's Center for Teaching Excellence, I am charged with offering programs that provide induction to new faculty. Almost all institutions have a similar center, one devoted to professional development of faculty.

New faculty need a planned induction program. Induction includes new faculty orientation, ongoing support seminars, and mentoring. Orientation provides the nuts and bolts of survival. Ongoing seminars may be informal brown bag seminars with discussion topics, or more formal seminars on timely topics. Topics in my seminar offerings have included the following:

1. Ten steps for starting the school year
2. How do I get students to read their assignments before class?
3. How do I get more students to participate in class?
4. Teaching the millennial students
5. Reaching first-year students
6. Staying positive in a tough academic year

I encourage new faculty to use mentors who are assigned to them by their department, and to also find their own mentors. How does a new person get the most out of their relationship with a mentor? Some keys include the following:

1. If you are assigned a mentor, find out the program's guidelines. Did your mentor volunteer? Get training? Or is he or she just assigned to answer an occasional question?
2. Get to know the mentor. Ask questions. Some mentors do not feel comfortable initiating a conversation about a topic, because you are already a highly qualified person, but they may be happy to share if you ask the question. (Remember to be considerate of their time, too.)

3. Set some time aside for coffee or lunch and talking. Good mentoring takes time and relationship building. You get what you invest.

Some people might call the first stage of teaching at an institution the survival stage. What should new people be doing for their own self-preservation at a job? All new hires need to make sure that they are meeting expectations to keep their jobs. They need to know about evaluations and how their teaching will be assessed. They need to start their publishing agendas and to learn how they need to serve the institution.

Networking is an excellent way to gain help with all three areas—teaching, writing, and serving. Keep in touch with former students in your doctoral programs as your professional network. Join professional organizations and attend their meetings. Get help from your former dissertation advisor about pulling one or two publishable articles from your dissertation research.

Is it hard to be a new person at a new institution? Yes, but the truth is it is hard to become established in any new job. Plan to spend a lot of time on lesson planning. Be prepared to work six days a week, although not necessarily on campus. It is very important to create a work schedule that works for you. Advice you will hear about the first couple of years may include the following:

1. Form a support group. This may be a group of three or four new people from across disciplines who meet once a month for lunch.
2. Find balance. It takes time to master teaching, to build professional networks, to serve the college, and to write your first articles. Allow time for doing so. Some people go so far as to say, "Don't start a family now or build a new house." These things are very personal choices, but remember that you can choose. One of the nice things about higher education is the flexibility we have in our work, as compared to some other professions.
3. Just say no. I hear a lot of professors tell new faculty "not to nickel and dime themselves to death." This means that they shouldn't accept every offer to help out with things that will take a lot of time but lead to little production. While it might be fun to advise two student groups, the time away from planning classes may not be worth it.
4. Don't say no every time. A dean was heard to remark at a professional meeting, "Not only do my new faculty say no assertively, they are down right blatant and rude about it." Being one of these people will not help your career.
5. Prioritize. Be ready to work hard and plan for good time management. Start early with projects. Make timelines. Remember that when the semester is the busiest, your chair may call a series of frantic meetings on budget cuts and curriculum reviews.
6. Don't make everything due late in the semester. Students need to have assignments spread out, and so do you.

The most important thing about being the new and enthused faculty member is that you are idealistic and ready to change the world, or at least to set it on fire. Don't apologize for your enthusiasm or the fact that you do work hard to teach classes. Find other positive colleagues and keep them close. This career stage is not necessarily one that you want to grow out of. You will lose your title of *new*, but hopefully not your label of *enthusiastic*.

Experienced

I am currently in my 12th year of teaching one of my classes and in my 8th year with another. I can say with certainty that experience helps dramatically with these two classes. Do I still change textbooks? Yes, and I still change tests and assignments, but the overall scope of the teaching is so much easier. It is nice to reach the experienced plateau. I tell people who have observed my classes that if they think I make teaching look easy, it is because I have been doing it the hard way for a long time.

How long does it take to be experienced? There is no timetable, and there is no way to say that after X years, you will feel comfortable and experienced. Also, if you have entered higher education from business or industry, where you were the experienced leader, it can be shocking to not feel experienced at this job. I once worked with a retired superintendent of schools who became an assistant professor. The man hired and fired hundreds of people and had a staff at his beck and call. When he asked about secretarial support at our college, we informed him that we all did our own word processing and that 15 of us shared one half-time secretary. It was a change. However, he quickly became experienced in his new job, as his background in his other position helped tremendously.

You may feel quite experienced as you approach time for tenure. Once tenured, you will probably feel quite relieved and very experienced. Achieving tenure is a big deal, and often brings with it a tremendous sense of job satisfaction. As a friend of mine said, "I'm so glad that I am no longer an assistant professor. That is such a misnomer. I never assisted anyone. When I was an assistant professor, my friends who didn't know higher ed thought that I was a teacher's aide, but in college. They didn't even realize it was a full-time job."

Earning tenure, or feeling that you have progressed to this experienced stage, will also bring with it more duties and responsibilities. Some departments add significant committee work to an employee's job after tenure or after three to five successful years in a position. Committees such as promotion and tenure and academic affairs carry with them heavy responsibilities and demand many clock hours of meetings.

What else changes with this stage? Many people look at the experienced stage as a time to actually increase their productivity. After earning tenure, I felt that I no longer had to produce articles just for lines on my résumé, or to meet the college's one-article-published-a-year requirement. I could put more time into fewer, but more significant publications. My writing of chapters, and of some books for teachers, became a priority.

What kinds of advice does an experienced college instructor hear? Well, some hear that they can slow down and pick and choose their committee work. Some people have actually been heard to say, "You are tenured; now you can just coast." Be wary of such negative advice. There are some college professors who never leave the experienced stage for the next one, the deep contributions stage. They stagnate and so do their courses. Some professors never strive to become full professors, content to teach their classes and spend their time on things other than writing.

On the positive side, professional development for experienced instructors and professors can be very productive. This is a time to get the most out of conferences, maybe adding international ones to your list. It is a time to experiment a little with your classes, adding more active learning or trying more technology. For some faculty, a sabbatical is available after tenure. A semester or a year to think, write, develop a project, travel, or invent a new course can be a wonderful thing. Once you have reached the experienced stage, decide on your new priorities and work toward your goals. In higher education we certainly do have many more opportunities than some of our teaching colleagues in K–12 schools or in the business world.

Deep Contributions

How does one get the title of professor? While every institution has its own set of guidelines, it generally means about, or at least, 12 years in the ranks of assistant or associate and significant contributions to the institution and to the discipline. In other words, continued strong teaching, research, writing, and service. Full professors should be ones who have contributed to the knowledge base in their discipline with the production of new knowledge. How exciting to work where we are producers of new knowledge, not just consumers of it.

Deep contributions to the institution and to the discipline can take many forms. You may chair committees that change policies. You may write materials that become the texts in courses across the country. You may teach state-of-the-art courses on your campus that help thousands of students.

What advice do those making deep contributions hear? They are often invited to sit on national committees, executive councils, or boards of directors. They may become speakers who are sought after for keynote addresses.

What kinds of professional development do you need at this stage of your career? One of my friends quipped that she just needed more time and more sleep! A sabbatical may be a pivotal step in a career at this stage. Getting the time to pursue the national or international venues to showcase your work or to learn about new research can invigorate your work back on campus.

We have all studied with, or worked with, professors who got to the stage of deep contributions, only to be completely burned out. Dealing with the bureaucracies of higher education, the budget cuts, the competition, and perhaps even the pettiness can wear a person down. What helps to prevent burnout in this stage? Some recommend outside interests, while others talk about changing something within your routine, such as a class or a research project.

A good way to stay connected and recharged is to keep good colleagues around you. Make those collegial friendships and keep them. Of course, they may not be on your campus. Many of us find that it is invaluable to have a network of friends who are not down the hall. We see them once or twice a year, e-mail them often, and while they can relate to our experiences, they are able to give us advice we might not get from someone in our own departments.

It is in the deep contributions stage that we also begin to mentor and truly help others in our profession. Advising doctoral candidates can be very rewarding, as can mentoring new faculty members. Lastly, your deep contributions to the institution may come in the form of administration. A strong department chair is actually a mentor, an advisor, a guide, and a facilitator. Good administrators see their roles as service and strive to get support for everyone within their department or program.

Is Administration for Me?

As instructors progress through their careers, they are often asked to assume administrative duties. Most commonly, they are asked to be department chairs. The duties of a department chair vary widely from institution to institution. In some colleges the chair has release time for the administrative duties and still teaches. In large universities the department chair is given a 12-month contract, and the duties of running the department do not permit any teaching.

Department chairs are charged with hiring, evaluating, and dismissing faculty members. They must observe faculty members' teaching, read their publications, and follow their service. The induction and mentoring of new faculty is often delegated to the department chair. When a faculty member becomes ill, the chair must determine how that professor's classes will be covered. The chair should be a guide in explaining the promotion and tenure process to new hires.

The chair is the person who must keep the whole department running and also supervises the support and secretarial staff.

Department chairs are in charge of programs. This may include completing class schedules and ensuring that all classes are offered when needed. They write and submit reports to provosts and presidents regarding majors and minors, and they are charged with keeping professional programs accredited. This involves attendance at national conferences and ongoing training from the accrediting agencies, such as ones in education, nursing, or business. The reports and paperwork can be tremendous.

Department chairs work one-on-one with students. They are often the judge for letting students register late for a full class, or for allowing a student to switch sections. They hear student complaints.

Budgets constitute a huge part of a department chair's duties. Supplies, equipment, and travel monies for faculty are increasingly expensive and budgets are rarely limitless.

Why do people accept the duties of being a department chair? Many professors become chairs because they believe in the service aspect of the position. Chairs can be advocates for people and programs, and chairs can get things done that support improvements for students. Many people accept a chair position as a stepping stone to a future administrative position—a deanship. Others take on the chair's duties because of increased pay, which can be significant.

After holding a department chair position, what might be next? The next logical step is usually a deanship. Deans are charged with running the school or college within the larger university setting. They supervise and evaluate the chairs, oversee all the programs and accreditations, and manage the bigger budgets. Of course, being the leader also means keeping morale high and providing vision for that branch of the institution. Deans are often charged with certain components of building security. A dean can be in charge of hundreds of faculty members and thousands of students. There is a lot of responsibility in a deanship.

So, why assume a deanship? The best reason to be a dean is to serve the institution. Strong deans provide leadership in both personnel and programs. They make the budgets work and keep morale high. A gifted dean is actually a recruitment tool to get high-quality faculty into the college. Being a dean is a way to increase one's salary and is a step to an administrative position that is campus wide, such as a provost's position or a vice presidency.

Provosts and college presidents are generally people who had fast-track, stellar faculty positions. They became noticed quickly for their work as chairs, deans, and college leaders. Many have planned to be college administrators since they decided to work in higher education. These are generally high-paying positions, but they are also very competitive ones. Mentoring and administrative internships have helped many provosts and presidents learn how to do their jobs.

There are many administrative positions on campuses that are not held by faculty or former faculty members. Business people are the vice presidents for finance and direct admissions and financial aid offices. People who have chosen a career in student personnel direct career centers, study abroad offices, and campus housing. These positions can pay quite well, often better than faculty positions. However, they are generally 12-month positions and require the regular 40-hour week. I know many PhDs who have left teaching to assume campus-wide positions as directors. Some made the change because they disliked the competitiveness of having to publish to keep their faculty position, or because they simply wanted to work in a different capacity. Some made the change for the increased pay of a 12-month contract.

If and when you seek an administrative position, or are invited to apply for one, how will you know if it is for you? Just as with starting your career in teaching, read widely about the job. Talk with those who are already doing similar jobs at your college and other institutions. Make sure that the expectations of the position are clearly stated and are within reason for one person to accomplish.

Many times faculty members do not have to change positions completely to assume some administrative duties. I have a contract that is one-fourth administrative and three-fourths teaching. I love what I do as the director of my campus' Center for Teaching Excellence, and I am certain that after a few years in the position I will know if I want to change to a full-time administrative position or not. The 10 percent addition to my salary was nice, too.

There is an old saying: "A prophet in his own land is without honor." Often, colleges spend tens of thousands of dollars on national searches to hire a new administrator who turns out to be not as qualified as a current faculty member. There is a time to simply step up and accept an administrative job as a new challenge. As you are building your career, do not hesitate to build some duties into your work that may open the door to administration to you.

Elder Statesperson

I currently work with two 70-year-old colleagues. Both continue to make valuable contributions through their teaching and committee work. They have progressed through the stages of new and enthusiastic, experienced, and deep contributions. In their own ways, both are still enthusiastic, keeping parts of that first stage throughout their careers. Eighteen-year-olds still respect them. In short, they are amazing and are my role models. How have they managed to work a lifetime in higher education and still be going strong?

The first answer is that they simply love what they do. They have both been professors for years, and teaching remains exciting for them. They are willing to grow and change with the times—adding technology to their teaching, teaming with younger colleagues, and recognizing that today's students are different in some respects than those of 30 years ago. Both are willing to speak up for students' rights, faculty rights, and the advancement of important college programs.

At my college, we often refer to some committee members as our institutional memory. It is hoped that all meetings are documented and changes are written into the faculty handbook in a timely manner, but the truth is that sometimes a person can relate a story that explains why we do things the way we do them better than committee minutes. I like to think that some faculty members grow into positions as elder statespersons just as Jimmy Carter continued to grow and contribute to society after his presidency.

Some faculty members grow into their elder statesperson role after they retire. They receive the professor emeritus title and continue to serve the institution. Some may speak at alumni events, and others may help with fund-raising. Occasionally, a professor emeritus may even be asked to serve on a board of trustees or board of visitors.

I don't have a crystal ball to predict my own career or that of anyone else. I do know that at each stage of a career, a person needs to have mentors, role models, and strong colleagues. It is imperative to keep reading, learning, and growing professionally. It can very helpful to use professional career counselors and life coaches. Getting away from one's own campus can provide invaluable rejuvenation. Conferences and travel help us to see the bigger picture of our profession and of our discipline.

In my years of college teaching, I have learned that teaching is not just stepping up to the lectern and talking. Good teaching is purposeful. It is explicit. It is planned. Teaching needs to be studied, practiced, and learned. It is a skill, and it can always be improved. People who enter higher education to be instructors, adjuncts, or professors all need to study the knowledge base of teaching. It is what we do, and we should want to improve our craft, for ourselves and for our students. We can improve our teaching at every stage of our career.

References

Anderson, L. W. (2003). *Classroom assessment: Enhancing the quality of teacher decision-making*. Mahwah, NJ: Lawrence Erlbaum.

Baldwin, M. D., Keating, J. F., & Bachman, K. J. (2006). *Teaching in secondary schools*. Upper Saddle River, NJ: Pearson.

Bart, M. (2009, November 9). "Managing Online Education" study sheds new light on the operations side of online programs. *Faculty Focus*. Available online at www.facultyfocus.com/articles/online-education.

Bok, D. (2006). *Our underachieving colleges*. Princeton, NJ: Princeton University Press.

Bonwell, C. C., & Eison, J. A. (1991). Active learning: Creating excitement in the classroom. Washington, DC: George Washington University.

Bonwell, C. C., & Sutherland, T. E. (1996, Fall). The active learning continuum: Choosing activities to engage students in the classroom. In T. E. Sutherland & C. C. Bonwell (Eds.), *Using active learning in college classrooms: A range of faculty options* (pp. 3–16). San Francisco: Jossey-Bass.

Bray, N. J., & Del Favero, M. (2004). Sociological explanations for faculty and student classroom incivilities. *New Directions for Teaching and Learning, 99*, 9–19.

Brookfield, S. D. (2006). *The skillful teacher*. San Francisco: Jossey-Bass.

Callahan, J. F., Clark, L. H., & Kellough, R. D. (2002). *Teaching in the middle and secondary schools* (7th ed.). Upper Saddle River, NJ: Merrill Prentice Hall.

Canter, L., & Canter, M. (1993). *Succeeding with difficult students*. Santa Monica, CA: Lee Canter and Associates.

Clement, M. C. (2005). *First time in the high school classroom: Essential guide for the new teacher*. Lanham, MD: Rowman & Littlefield Education.

Clement, M. C. (2008). *How to interview, hire, and retain high-quality new teachers* (2nd ed.). Alexandria, VA: Educational Research Service.

Davis, B. G. (2009). *Tools for teaching* (2nd ed.). San Francisco: Jossey-Bass.

Eggen, P. D., & Kauchak, D. P. (2006). *Strategies and models for teachers: Teaching content and thinking skills* (5th ed.). Boston: Pearson.

Feldman, L. J. (2001). Classroom civility is another of our instructor responsibilities. *College Teaching, 49*(4), 137–140.

Fredericks, A. D. (2007). *The complete idiot's guide to teaching college.* New York: Alpha.

Gabler, I. C., & Schroeder, M. (2003). *Constructivist methods for the secondary classroom: Engaged minds.* Boston: Allyn & Bacon.

Gabriel, K. F. (2008). *Teaching unprepared students.* Sterling, VA: Stylus.

Gainer, B. L. (2008, November). Using MySpace to build community in college. *Teaching Professor, 22*(9), 5.

Gappa, J. M., Austin, A. E., & Trice, A. G. (2007). *Rethinking faculty work.* San Francisco: Jossey-Bass.

Gilroy, M. (2008). Colleges grappling with incivility. *Education Digest, 74*(4), 36–40.

Glickman, C. D., Gordon, S. P., & Ross-Gordon, J. M. (2008). *The basic guide to supervision and instructional leadership* (2nd ed.). Boston: Pearson.

Hirschy, A. S., & Braxton, J. M. (2004). Effects of student classroom incivilities on students. *New Directions for Teaching and Learning, 99.*

Howe, N., & Strauss, W. (2007). *Millennials go to college: Strategies for a new generation on campus.* Great Falls, VA: LifeCourse Associates.

Hunter, M. (1994). *Enhancing teaching.* New York: Macmillan College.

Indiana University Center for Survey Research. (2000). *A survey on academic incivility at Indiana University.* Bloomington, IN: Author. Available online at www.indiana.edu/~csr/Civility%20PreReport.pdf.

Jones, F., Jones, P., Jones, J. L., & Jones, B. T. (2007). *Tools for teaching.* Santa Cruz, CA: Fredric H. Jones.

Kagan, S. (1995, May). Group grades miss the mark. *Educational Leadership, 52*(8), 68–71.

Kellough, R. D., & Carjuzaa, J. (2006). *Teaching in the middle and secondary schools* (8th ed.). Upper Saddle River, NJ: Pearson/Merrill Prentice Hall.

Kellough, R. D., & Kellough, N. G. (2003). *Secondary school teaching: A guide to methods and resources: Planning for competence* (2nd ed.). Upper Saddle River, NJ: Merrill Prentice Hall.

Kelly, Rob. (2009, July 1). Creating an online presence for your online students. *Faculty Focus.* Available online at www.facultyfocus.com/articles/online-education/page/3/.

Lang, J. M. (2005). *Life on the tenure track: Lessons from the first year.* Baltimore: Johns Hopkins University Press.

Lang, J. M. (2008). *On course: A week-by-week guide to your first semester of college teaching.* Cambridge, MA: Harvard University Press.

Lefebvre, N. (2006). Leaving "school" out of high school. *Education Next, 6*(3), 88.

Lieberg, C. (2008). *Teaching your first college class.* Sterling, VA: Stylus.

Linder, K. (2009). Students and social networking: Should you "friend" your students? Available online at www.facultyfocus.com/articles/trends-in-higher-education.

Linehan, P. (2007). *Win them over: Techniques for college adjuncts and new faculty.* Madison, WI: Atwood Publishing.

Martin, J. R. (2007). There's too much to teach. In A. C. Ornstein, E. F. Pajak, & S. B. Ornstein (Eds.), *Contemporary issues in curriculum* (pp. 39–50). Boston: Pearson/Allyn & Bacon.

Marzano, R. J. (2009). Setting the record straight on "high yield" strategies. *Phi Delta Kappan, 91*(1), 30–37.

McGlynn, A. P. (2001). *Successful beginnings for college teaching*. Madison, WI: Atwood Publishing.

McKeachie, W. J. (1994). *Teaching tips* (9th ed.). Lexington, MA: D. C. Heath.

McKeachie, W. J., & Svinicki, M. (2006). *Teaching tips* (12th ed.). Boston: Houghton Mifflin.

Moore, K. D. (2005). *Effective instructional strategies: From theory to practice*. Thousand Oaks, CA: Sage Publications.

Nordstrom, C. R., Bartels, L. K., & Bucy, J. (2009). Predicting and curbing classroom incivility in higher education. *College Student Journal, 43*(1). Retrieved online Academic Search Complete.

Norin, L., & Walton, T. (n.d.). A behavior contract that made a difference. In *Faculty Focus special report: 10 effective classroom management techniques every faculty member should know*. Madison, WI: Magna Publications. Available online at www.faculty focus.com.

Ornstein, A. C., Lasley II, T. J., & Mindes, G. (2005). *Secondary and middle school methods*. Boston: Pearson/Allyn & Bacon.

Pink, D. H. (2005). *A whole new mind*. New York: Riverhead Books.

Ragan, L. C. (2009). 10 principles of effective online teaching: Best practices in distance education. In *Faculty Focus special report*. Madison, WI: Magna Publications. Available online at www.facultyfocus.com.

Shulman, L. (2007). Knowledge and teaching: Foundations of the new reform. In A. C. Ornstein, E. F. Pajak, & S. B. Ornstein (Eds.), *Contemporary issues in curriculum* (pp. 113–131). Boston: Pearson/Allyn & Bacon.

Silver, H. F., Strong, R. W., & Perini, M. J. (2007). *The strategic teacher: Selecting the right research-based strategy for every lesson*. Upper Saddle River, NJ: Merrill Prentice Hall.

Smelter, R. W. (2009). Backtalk: Is college the new high school? *Phi Delta Kappan, 90*(6), 456.

Steffy, B. E. (1989). *Career stages of classroom teachers*. Lancaster, PA: Technomic.

Steffy, B. E., Wolfe, M. P., Pasch, S. H., & Enz, B. J. (2000). *Life cycle of the career teacher*. Indianapolis, IN: Kappa Delta Pi.

Twenge, J. M. (2006). *Generation me*. New York: Free Press.

Vick, J. M., & Furlong, J. S. (2008). *The academic job search handbook*. Philadelphia: University of Pennsylvania Press.

Weimer, M. (2002). *Learner-centered teaching: Five key changes to practice*. San Francisco: Jossey-Bass.

Weimer, M. (n.d.). Those students who participate too much. In *Faculty Focus special report: 10 effective classroom management techniques every faculty member should know*. Madison, WI: Magna Publications. Available online at www.facultyfocus.com.

Wong, H. K., & Wong, R. T. (1991). *The first days of school: How to be an effective teacher*. Mountain View, CA: Harry K. Wong Publications.

Wong, H. K., & Wong, R. T. (1998). *The first days of school: How to be an effective teacher*. Mountain View, CA: Harry K. Wong Publications.

Website Resources

Beloit College Mindset List: www.beloit.edu/mindset/2011.php
The Chronicle of Higher Education: www.chronicle.com
Derek Bok Center for Learning and Teaching: http://bokcenter.harvard.edu/icb/icb.do
Faculty Focus: www.facultyfocus.com
Rubistar.com: www.rubistar.com

Index

About the Author

Mary C. Clement was a high school foreign language teacher for eight years before earning her doctorate in curriculum and instruction from the University of Illinois at Urbana-Champaign. She directed the Beginning Teacher Program at Eastern Illinois University for six years. She is currently a professor of education at Berry College, northwest of Atlanta, Georgia, where she also directs the college's Center for Teaching Excellence.

Clement is the author of seven books, including *The Definitive Guide to Getting a Teaching Job*, *Building the Best Faculty*, and *How to Interview, Hire, and Retain High-Quality New Teachers*. Her articles have appeared in the *Kappan*, *Academic Leader*, *School Administrator*, *Principal Leadership*, and the *American School Board Journal*.

Breinigsville, PA USA
01 June 2010
238936BV00002B/1/P